Das einzig authentische Porträt des Alten Frit

Entdeckt in Hogarths *Marriage A-la-Mode*

von

BERND KRYSMANSKI

Is the only true likeness of Frederick the Great
to be found in Hogarth's *Marriage A-la-Mode*?

2015

Cover-Illustrationen
Vorderseite:
Simon François Ravenet nach William Hogarth: *Marriage A-la-Mode,*
Plate 4. Radierung u. Kupferstich, 1745. Ausschnitt.
Rückseite:
Daniel Chodowiecki: *Frédéric II. Roi de Prusse.* Radierung, 1777.
Ausschnitt.

Die Deutsche Nationalbibliothek verzeichnet diese Publikation in der
Deutschen Nationalbibliografie. Detaillierte bibliografische Daten
sind im Internet unter http://dnb.d-nb.de abrufbar.

Cover-Design Dipl.-Des. Markus Ceh, Essen
Herstellung Bernd Krysmanski und Markus Ceh
Druck Jelgavas Tipogrāfija, Jelgava, Lettland
Alle Rechte vorbehalten.
Printed in Latvia
© Krysman Press, Dinslaken 2015
ISBN 978-3-00-050343-6

Inhalt

Die mangelnde Schönheit Friedrichs des Großen

Friedrich der Große mochte sein Antlitz nicht. Er wollte sich nicht im Spiegel sehen und verabscheute die meisten seiner Porträts. Der Grund: Er selbst empfand sich als potthässlich! Die Totenmaske, die dem verstorbenen Preußenkönig von Johann Eckstein am 17. August 1786 abgenommen wurde,[1] offenbart es allzu deutlich: Der Alte Fritz hatte eine Adlernase und auch sonst keine attraktiven Gesichtszüge, die man mit einem klassischen Schönheitsideal in Übereinstimmung bringen könnte.

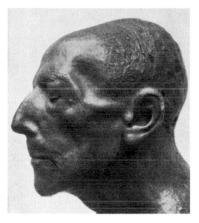

Totenmaske Friedrichs des Großen (1786)

Dies bestätigt auch der selbsternannte Physiognomik-Experte Johann Caspar Lavater, als er Friedrich den Großen, nachdem er ihn aus der Nähe gesehen hatte, als „Nicht auf die Art schön, wie unphysiognomische Maler ihn idealisieren – nicht auf die Art groß! – ganz und gar nicht schön" beschrieb.[2] Friedrich selbst war sich seiner äußerlichen Mängel wohl bewusst. Zum Marquis d'Argens bemerkte er: „Man spricht so viel darüber, dass wir Könige das Ebenbild Gottes auf Erden sind. Darauf habe ich mich im Spie-

---

1 Vgl. zur Totenmaske: Friedrich Benninghoven/Helmut Börsch-Supan/Iselin Grundermann: *Friedrich der Grosse: Ausstellung des Geheimen Staatsarchivs Preußischer Kulturbesitz anläßlich des 200. Todestages König Friedrichs II. von Preußen* (Berlin: Nicolai 1986), XIV, 327–28; Johann Georg Prinz von Hohenzollern: *Friedrich der Große: Sammler und Mäzen* (München: Hirmer Verlag 1992), 392; Hans-Joachim Neumann: *Friedrich der Große: Feldherr und Philosoph* (Berlin: Ed. q. 2000), 230, 232; Wilhelm Bringmann: *Friedrich der Große: Ein Porträt* (München: Herbert Utz Verlag 2006), 34.

2 Johann Caspar Lavater: *Physiognomische Fragmente zur Beförderung von Menschenkenntnis und Menschenliebe*, 4 Bände (Leipzig und Winterthur: Weidmanns Erben und Reich; Heinrich Steiner und Compagnie 1775–1778), Dritter Versuch, 348.

gel besehen und muss sagen: Desto schlimmer für Gott!"[3] Doch er nahm's mit bissigem Humor. Über seine markante Nase pflegte er zu sagen: „Ich habe eine große Nase, aber sie ist nicht da, um auf ihr herumzutanzen."[4] Da der Preußenkönig, je älter er wurde, auch kleidungsmäßig seine äußere Erscheinung immer mehr vernachlässigte, musste sich eines Tages sein Vorleser und Privatsekretär Henri de Catt folgende Bemerkung von ihm anhören: „Sehe ich nicht ein bisschen wie ein Schwein aus?"[5]

Die idealisierenden Bildnisse

Nur die Personen aus seinem engeren Umfeld kannten das wahre Aussehen des Monarchen, denn auf offiziellen Porträts wurde gemogelt, was der Pinsel hergab. Keines der existierenden Bildnisse zeigt Friedrich den Großen so, wie er wirklich ausgesehen hat. Im Gegenteil: Fast alle geben ihn stark idealisiert wieder, vielleicht mit Ausnahme einiger Altersporträts. Münzen, wie sie etwa 1740 zur Thronbesteigung und auch noch später herausgegeben wurden, lassen eine genauere Porträtähnlichkeit ebenso vermissen wie die gemalten Bildnisse derselben Zeit. Fast all diese Darstellungen sind mehr oder weniger frei erfunden, denn üblicherweise ließ der Monarch keine Bildnismaler an sich ran.

Antoine Pesne: *Kronprinz Friedrich* (1736)   Antoine Pesne: *Kronprinz Friedrich* (1738)

---

3 Gisela Groth: "Wie Friedrich II. wirklich aussah", *Preußische Allgemeine Zeitung*, 14 November 2012.

4 *Allgemeine Zeitung*, no. 362 (28 December 1854), 5784.

5 Wilhelm Bringmann: *Preußen unter Friedrich Wilhelm II. (1786–1797)* (Frankfurt am Main: Peter Lang 2001), 104.

Antoine Pesne: *Friedrich der Große* (1745)   Antoine Pesne: *Friedrich der Große* (1746)

Georg Wenzeslaus von Knobelsdorff: Medaille auf die Siege des Jahres 1757
Kronprinz Friedrich (um 1737; Pastell)

Er hielt sich nicht für porträtwürdig, weil er, wie er selbst einräumte, keinerlei Ähnlichkeit mit Apollo, Mars oder Adonis hatte.[6] 1743 schrieb er seinem Freund Voltaire, der nach einem aktuellen Bildnis von ihm gefragt hatte:

---

6 „Man muß Apollo, Mars oder Adonis sein, um sich malen zu lassen, da ich nun aber nicht die Ehre habe, einem dieser Herren zu gleichen, so habe ich mein Antlitz, soviel es von mir abhing, dem Pinsel der Maler entzogen", schrieb Friedrich am 14. Dezember 1774 an Jean-Baptiste le Rond d'Alembert. Zitiert bei Hans Dollinger: *Friedrich II. von Preußen: Sein Bild im Wandel von zwei Jahrhunderten* (München: List Verlag 1986), 82; Andrea M. Kluxen: *Bild eines Königs: Friedrich der Große in der Graphik* (Limburg/Lahn: C. A. Starke 1986), 28.

„Ich bin nicht gemalt, lasse mich auch nicht malen und kann Ihnen also nichts geben als Medaillen."[7]

Thomas Burford: *Frederick II*   Antoine Benoist: *Frederick III*[d]

Was natürlich nicht ganz stimmte, denn es gab ja einige Porträts von ihm, zumal die Nachfrage nach seinem Konterfei an allen europäischen Höfen recht hoch war. Doch konnten die Künstler, wenn überhaupt, das Erscheinungsbild des Königs für diese Bildnisse allenfalls aus einiger Entfernung grob erfassen. Und sie verpassten dem jüngeren Preußenkönig, um ihm zu schmeicheln, meist viel zu glatte Gesichtszüge und eine klassisch begradigte Nase, bei der sich der Nasenrücken in gerader Linie bis in die Stirn hinein fortsetzt. Besonders deutlich wird dies in reinen Profilansichten, etwa im Pastell von Georg Wenzeslaus von Knobelsdorff, das den Kopf des Kronprinzen von der rechten Seite zeigt.[8] Zudem wurden nicht selten einmal ent-

---

7 Karl Heinrich Siegfried Rödenbeck: *Tagebuch oder Geschichtskalender aus Friedrich's des Großen Regentenleben (1740–1786)*, Band 1 (Berlin: Verlag der Plahn'schen Buchhandlung 1840), 92.

8 Siehe Ute-G. Weickardt/Tigo Eggeling (Hrsg.): *„Zum Maler und zum Großen Architekten geboren": Georg Wenzeslaus von Knobelsdorff. 1699–1753*, Katalog zur Ausstellung zum 300. Geburtstag, 18. Februar–25 April 1999 (Berlin: Generaldirektion der Stiftung Preußische Schlösser und Gärten Berlin-Brandenburg 1999), 170; Benninghoven/Börsch-Supan/Grundermann: *Friedrich der Grosse*, 32. Zur Ölversion dieses Profilbildnisses: Paul Seidel: *Friedrich der Grosse und die bildende Kunst* (Leipzig und Berlin: Giesecke & Devrient 1922), 39–40. Siehe auch Helmut Börsch-Supan: "Bemerkungen zu einem wiedergefundenen Bildnis Friedrichs des Großen von Georg Wenzeslaus von Knobelsdorff", in: Lucius Grisebach/Konrad Renger (Hrsg.): *Festschrift für Otto von Simson zum 65. Geburtstag* (Frankfurt am Main: Propyläen Verlag 1977), 398–411.

standene, bekannt gewordene Porträts, z.B. die Bruststücke von Antoine Pesne, immer wieder als Vorlage benutzt.[9] Auch die in ganz Europa verbreiteten Porträt-Stiche von Georg Friedrich Schmidt, Johann Georg Wille, Antoine Benoist oder Thomas Burford zeigen das Antlitz des jüngeren Friedrich in einer zu stark verallgemeinernden und idealisierten Form ohne Adlernase.

Johann Georg Ziesenis: *Friedrich der Große* (1763). Ausschnitt.

Johann Heinrich Christian Franke: *Friedrich II., den Hut ziehend* (1764)

Ja, wenn man einige dieser Porträts direkt miteinander vergleicht, fällt es einem schon schwer zu glauben, dass auf ihnen jeweils die gleiche Person dargestellt sein soll. Das natürliche Aussehen Friedrichs repräsentieren sie nicht. Interessant ist auch, dass der Monarch selbst mit den geschönten Bildnissen, die seine Verwandten in Auftrag gegeben hatten, nicht recht zufrieden war. Seinem Neffen Prinz Friedrich August von Braunschweig-Wolfenbüttel, der eines dieser ungeliebten Porträts für seine Freimaurerloge bestellt hatte, empfahl er, das Bild lieber als Vogelscheuche zu verwenden![10]

---

9 Vgl. Helmut Börsch-Supan: *Der Maler Antoine Pesne: Franzose und Preusse* (Friedberg: Podzun-Pallas 1986); ders.: *Die Gemälde Antoine Pesnes in den Berliner Schlössern* (Berlin: Verwaltung der Staatlichen Schlösser und Gärten 1982) [*Aus Berliner Schlossern*, 7]; ders.: "Friedrich der Große im zeitgenössischen Bildnis", in: Oswald Hauser (Hrsg.): *Friedrich der Große in seiner Zeit* (Köln und Wien: Böhlau Verlag 1987), 255–270; Gerd Bartoschek: *Antoine Pesne, 1683–1757: Ausstellung zum 300. Geburtstag*, Kat. der Ausstellung im Neuen Palais und in den Römischen Bädern Potsdam-Sanssouci, Juni–September 1983, und im Märkischen Museum Berlin, Oktober–Dezember 1983 (Potsdam-Sanssouci: Generaldirektion der Staatlichen Schlösser und Gärten 1983).

10 Siehe Reinhold Koser: *Geschichte Friedrichs des Großen*, 4 Bände, 4. und 5. vermehrte Auflage (Stuttgart: J. G. Cotta 1912–1913), Band 3, 528; Martin Schieder: "Die auratische Abwesenheit des Königs: Zum schwierigen Umgang Friedrichs des Großen mit dem eigenen Bildnis", in: Bernd Sösemann/Gregor Vogt-Spira (Hrsg.): *Friedrich der Große in Europa: Geschichte einer wechselvollen Beziehung*, 2 Bände (Stuttgart: Franz Steiner Verlag 2012), Band I, 331.

Abgesehen von einer Porträt-Miniatur des 21jährigen Kronprinzen, die 1733 von Pesne ausgeführt wurde,[11] soll das einzige Bildnis, für das Friedrich angeblich wenige Stunden Modell gesessen hat, von seinem Hofmaler Johann Georg Ziesenis 1763 gemalt worden sein.[12] Doch konnte in neueren Untersuchungen nicht zweifelsfrei nachgewiesen werden, ob es für dieses „spießbürgerliche" Bildnis tatsächlich Porträtsitzungen gab.[13] Fest steht nur, dass es von Philippine Charlotte von Braunschweig-Wolfenbüttel, der Schwester des Monarchen, in Auftrag gegeben wurde. Es zeigt den König wie üblich ohne Hakennase und mit verhalten-freundlicher Miene, ist also ebenfalls ein stark idealisiertes Porträt, weshalb man auch bei diesem Gemälde von einer „glaubwürdigen" Darstellung Friedrichs kaum sprechen kann, obwohl dies gelegentlich behauptet wurde.

Realistischere Altersporträts und Menzels Querflöte spielender Friedrich

Unkonventioneller und schnörkelloser – eben bürgerlicher – (und mit der Hand seinen Dreispitz ziehend) erscheint der Porträtierte wenig später nur auf Johann Heinrich Christian Frankes Bildnis von 1763/64[14] sowie – in leicht gebeugter Haltung zu Pferde – auf der 1772 entstandenen Gouache von Daniel Chodowiecki (die wenige Jahre später auch als Vorlage für eine Stichversion diente)[15] und – als gütig dreinschauender alter Monarch, so wie ihn der Künstler bei einer Parade beobachtet hatte – auf dem 1781 gemalten, oft kopierten Gemälde von Anton Graff (Schloss Charlottenburg).[16]

---

11 Siehe Rainer Michaelis: "Kronprinz Friedrich von Preußen en miniature: Notizen zu einer Arbeit Antoine Pesnes", *Pantheon* 54 (1996), 190–192.

12 Näheres hierzu bei Jean Lulvès: *Das einzige glaubwürdige Bildnis Friedrichs des Großen als König* (Hannover und Leipzig: Hahn 1913); August Fink: "Herzogin Philippine Charlotte und das Bildnis Friedrichs des Großen", *Braunschweigisches Jahrbuch* 40 (1959), 117–135.

13 Siehe Karin Schrader: *Der Bildnismaler Johann Georg Ziesenis (1717–1776): Leben und Werk mit kritischem Oeuvrekatalog* (Münster: LIT Verlag 1995), 110.

14 Dieses und ähnliche Gemälde zählen zu den populärsten Darstellungen des Preußenkönigs. Sie haben das volkstümliche Friedrich-Bild wohl am nachhaltigsten geprägt. Siehe auch Johann Georg Prinz von Hohenzollern: *Friedrich der Große: Sammler und Mäzen*, 382–383 und Abb. 1. Vgl. ferner den Kupferstich von Eduard Mandel (1860) nach Frankes Kniestück von 1770, abgebildet in Veit Veltzke (Hrsg.): *Macht und Dienst: Zur Darstellung des brandenburgisch-preußischen Herrscherhauses in Gemälde und Graphik 1650–1900*, Ausst.-Kat., Städtische Galerie im Centrum Wesel, 17. Oktober–7. November 1993; Schloss Cappenberg, 25. November 1993–27. Februar 1994 (Minden und Wesel: Preußen-Museum Nordrhein-Westfalen 1993), 100.

15 Zu Chodowieckis Friedrich-Darstellungen: Paul Dehnert: "Daniel Chodowiecki und der König", *Jahrbuch Preussischer Kulturbesitz* 14 (1977), 307–319; Johann Georg Prinz von Hohenzollern: *Friedrich der Große: Sammler und Mäzen*, 112; Rainer Michaelis: "Friedrich der Große im Spiegel der Werke des Daniel Nikolaus Chodowiecki", in: *Friederisiko: Friedrich der Große*, Ausst.-Kat., Stiftung Preußische Schlösser und Gärten Berlin-Brandenburg im Neuen Palais und Park Sanssouci, 28. April–28. Oktober 2012, 2 Bände (München: Hirmer 2012), Band II: *Die Essays*, 262–271.

16 Siehe Ekhart Berckenhagen: *Anton Graff: Leben und Werk* (Berlin: Deutscher Verlag für Kunstwissen-

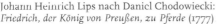

Johann Heinrich Lips nach Daniel Chodowiecki: *Friedrich, der König von Preußen, zu Pferde* (1777)

Anton Graff: *Friedrich der Große* (1781)

Den berittenen Friedrich aus der Stichversion von Johann Heinrich Lips nach Chodowiecki[17] übernahm Lavater 1777 als Illustration für seine *Physiognomischen Fragmente*, weil er der Ansicht war, dass hier „der Große, Er selber, vorbey ritt", wie er ihn in natura kannte: "weg auf einmal alle Bilder von ihm! [...] So war er [...] (so fern's Kleinheit und Nadel und Einbildungskraft des Zeichners erreichen mag!) [...] und nicht wie Wille ihn herrlich metallisierte."[18] Dennoch erscheint die Nase des Königs selbst hier in begradigter Form. Schließlich war es mit Lavaters Menschenbild unvereinbar, dass der Preußenkönig eine krumme Nase haben könnte.[19]

Da es – vielleicht mit Ausnahme der nicht autorisierten Altersporträts – keine wahrhaft authentischen Friedrich-Porträts aus dem 18. Jahrhundert gab, die dem tatsächlichen Aussehen des Monarchen nahe kamen, konnte

schaft 1967), 119; Robert Eberhardt (Hrsg.): *Anton Graff: Porträts eines Porträtisten* (Berlin: Wolff 2013); Marc Fehlmann/Birgit Verwiebe (Hrsg.): *Anton Graff: Gesichter einer Epoche* (München: Hirmer 2013).

17 Siehe *Fridericus-Stiche: Eine Hommage an Friedrich den Grossen von Heinrich von Sydow-Zirkwitz für die Friderizianische Gesellschaft zu Berlin* (Frankfurt am Main: Edition Sydow 1986), 84; Joachim Kruse: *Johann Heinrich Lips, 1758–1817: Ein Zürcher Kupferstecher zwischen Lavater und Goethe* (Coburg: Die Kunstsammlungen der Veste Coburg 1989) [*Kataloge der Kunstsammlungen der Veste Coburg*, Nr. 54], 84–85.

18 Lavater: *Physiognomische Fragmente zur Beförderung von Menschenkenntnis und Menschenliebe*, Dritter Versuch, 348. Mit „Wille" ist der damals in Paris wirkende Kupferstecher Johann Georg Wille gemeint.

19 So ist es für Lavater unvorstellbar, dass man ein Profil von Christus mit einer eingedrückten oder einer „Habichtsnase" erträglich finden könne. Siehe Johann Caspar Lavater: *Von der Physiognomik: Zweytes Stück, welches einen in allen Absichten sehr unvollkommnen Entwurf zu einem Werke von dieser Art enthält*, Band 2 (Leipzig: bey Weidmanns Erben und Reich 1772), 116, Anm.

auch Adolph Menzel im 19. Jahrhundert für seine berühmte Darstellung des *Flötenkonzerts in Sanssouci* (1850/52; Nationalgalerie Berlin)[20] nicht auf eine geeignete Vorlage zurückgreifen, die das Antlitz des preußischen Königs in seinen jüngeren Lebensjahren korrekt wiedergab. So meinte denn auch ein Betrachter aus unseren Tagen zur Hauptfigur auf diesem Bild: „Das ist doch niemals der Alte Fritz, das ist Mozart!" Auch wenn es dieser Betrachter kaum glauben konnte, es handelt sich bei dem Berliner Gemälde in der Tat um Menzels Version eines privaten Abendkonzerts Friedrichs des Großen, wobei das Flötenspiel des Monarchen zu einem Event vor hohen Gästen monumentalisiert wurde, und zwar in einer bis ins Detail nachempfundenen Kerzenlicht-Atmosphäre, die „Rokoko-Feeling" aufkommen lässt. Der Preußenkönig erscheint zwar in einer realistisch gemalten, aber dennoch verklärt-idealisierten Form, so dass es verständlich ist, dass der Flötenspieler bei flüchtiger, uninformierter Betrachtung für Mozart gehalten werden kann. Typisch auch, dass Menzel den Musiker Friedrich wie selbstverständlich wieder mit einem begradigten Nasenrücken darstellt.

Hogarths homosexueller Friedrich

Gibt es denn gar kein Friedrich-Porträt, auf dem die Hakennase als charakteristisches Merkmal hervorsticht? Doch, eine solche Darstellung gibt es, allerdings an höchst unvermuteter Stelle und in einem satirischen Zusammenhang, so dass das Motiv bis heute unentdeckt geblieben ist: Es stammt vom englischen Maler und Kupferstecher William Hogarth (1697–1764), der im 18. Jahrhundert mit „modernen", satirisch-sarkastischen Sujets Furore machte. In Szene 4 seiner berühmten sechsteiligen Bilderserie *Marriage A-la-Mode* (1743/44; National Gallery, London; Stichversion 1745),[21]

---

20 Siehe Günther Thiersch: "Das Flötenkonzert", in: *Deutsche Maler im 19. Jahrhundert: Zwanzig Meisterwerke aus dem Besitz der Nationalgalerie Berlin, Staatliche Museen Preußischer Kulturbesitz* (Stuttgart: Ernst Klett 1979), 130–140; Jost Hermand: *Adolph Menzel: Das Flötenkonzert in Sanssouci. Ein realistisch geträumtes Preußenbild* (Frankfurt am Main: Fischer Taschenbuch Verlag 1985).

21 Zur Serie: Christoph Lichtenberg: *Schriften und Briefe*, Band III: *Aufsätze, Entwürfe, Gedichte, Erklärung der Hogarthischen Kupferstiche*, hrsg. von Wolfgang Promies (München: Carl Hanser Verlag 1972), 913–989; Ronald Paulson: *Hogarth: His Life, Art, and Times*, 2 Bände (New Haven und London: Yale University Press 1971), Band I, 465–497; Band II, 122–126; ders.: *The Art of Hogarth* (London: Phaidon Press 1975), 30–40; ders.: *Hogarth's Graphic Works*, 3. Aufl. (London: The Print Room 1989), 114–124; ders.: *Hogarth, Volume 2: High Art and Low, 1732–1750* (Cambridge: Lutterworth Press 1992), 208–245; Robert L. S. Cowley: *Marriage A-la-Mode: a re-view of Hogarth's narrative art* (Manchester: Manchester University Press 1983); Judy Egerton: *National Gallery Catalogues: The British School* (London: National Gallery Publications, Distributed by Yale University Press 1998); dies.: *Hogarth's 'Marriage A-la-Mode'*, Ausst.-Kat., The National Gallery, London, 15. Oktober 1997–18. Januar 1998; dies.: "Zu William Hogarths Zyklus *Marriage A-la-Mode*", in: *'Marriage A-la-Mode' – Hogarth und seine deutschen Bewunderer*, Ausst.-Kat., Staatliche Museen zu Berlin, Nationalgalerie – Altes Museum, Berlin, 18. Dezember 1998–28. Februar 1999, Städelsches Kunstinstitut und Städtische Galerie Frankfurt am Main, 25. März–20. Juni 1999, hrsg. von Martina

die einen beim Hochadel damals üblichen Morgenempfang im Schlaf-
zimmer der Gräfin Squander zeigt, taucht Friedrich als Flötenspieler hinter einem singenden italienischen Kastraten und vor einem an der Wand
hängenden Bild auf, das – nach Michelangelo – eine homoerotische Szene darstellt, nämlich Jupiter in Gestalt eines Adlers, wie er den Jüngling
Ganymed, in den er sich unsterblich verliebt hatte, zum Olymp entführt.[22]

Adolph Menzel: *Das Flötenkonzert in
Sanssouci* (1850/52). Ausschnitt.

Simon François Ravenet nach William Hogarth:
Marriage A-la-Mode, Plate 4 (1745). Ausschnitt.

Doch was hat Friedrich der Große auf Hogarths Bild zu suchen? Zunächst
einmal sei darauf verwiesen, dass das Bild einen Ehebruch zeigt: Die Dame
des Hauses, die gerade frisiert wird, flirtet nämlich heftig mit ihrem Liebhaber, der sie zu einem erotischen Maskeradenball einlädt. Ihr Gatte schlürft
derweil auf der anderen Bildseite gänzlich desinteressiert ein Tässchen

Dillmann und Claude Keisch (Berlin: Staatliche Museen zu Berlin – Preussischer Kulturbesitz 1998), 22–
68; Mark Hallett: "Foreign Affairs: *Marriage à la Mode*", in: ders.: *Hogarth* (London: Phaidon Press 2000),
165–196; Christine Riding: "Marriage A-la-Mode", in: Mark Hallett/Christine Riding: *Hogarth*, Ausst.-Kat.
Musée du Louvre, Paris, 18. Oktober 2006–7. Januar 2007; Tate Britain, London, 7. Februar–29. April
2007; Caixa Forum, Barcelona, 29. Mai–26. August 2007 (London: Tate Publishing 2006), 140–157; Bernd
Krysmanski: "Der pädophile Adelsspross: Warum die arrangierte Ehe 'nach der Mode' scheitern musste.
Eine Neubewertung von Hogarths *Marriage A-la-Mode* aus sexualgeschichtlicher Sicht zum 250jährigen
Todestag des Künstlers", *Lichtenberg-Jahrbuch 2013* (Heidelberg: Universitätsverlag Winter 2015), 57–141;
Elizabeth Einberg: *The Paintings of William Hogarth: A Catalogue Raisonné* (New Haven und London: Pub-
lished for the Paul Mellon Centre for Studies in British Art by Yale University Press. In Vorbereitung).

22 Hogarth könnte für sein Bild im Bild den Nachstich von Quirin Bol nach einer verschollenen Mi-
chelangelo-Zeichnung genutzt haben. Vgl. Cowley: *Marriage A-la-Mode*, 114–115 und Abb. 30 a–d.

heiße Schokolade. Durch die Lockenwickler im Haar und die gehörnte Ac-
taeon-Figur, die in einem Korb mit diversen Auktionsgegenständen steckt
und auf die augenzwinkernd ein farbiger Junge deutet, wird er satirisch
zu einem mehrfach gehörnten Ehemann degradiert. Doch nicht nur das:
Hogarth macht mit seinem Figurenarrangement deutlich, dass die Gäste
und Gastgeber des Morgenempfangs bezüglich ihrer sexuellen Bedürfnisse
zweigeteilt sind: Während die eine Bildseite quasi die Gräfin und ihren
willig vollzogenen Ehebruch beschreibt, auf den auch ein Gemälde an der
Wand anspielt, nämlich Correggios nackte, verzückte *Io* (ca. 1530; Kunsthistorisches Museum, Wien), wie sie von Jupiter in Gestalt eines grauen Nebels
umarmt wird, gehört die andere Bildseite den Vertretern ganz anderer sexu-
eller Geschmacksrichtungen, die eines gemeinsam haben: die Vorliebe für
Kinder oder das eigene Geschlecht.

Simon François Ravenet nach William Hogarth: *Marriage A-la-Mode,*
Plate 4 (1745). Ausschnitt.

Simon François Ravenet nach William
Hogarth: *Marriage A-la-Mode,* Plate 4
(1745). Ausschnitt.

Zu ihnen zählt der an ehelichen Sexualkontakten nicht interessierte und von
Homosexuellen umrahmte, pädophile Lord, auf dessen wahre sexuelle Neigungen nicht nur die vorhergehende Szene, die ihn mit einer minderjähri-
gen Hure zeigt, sondern auch der am Boden liegende Auktionskatalog eines
gewissen „S[i]r Tim[oth]y Babyhouse" verweist.[23] Der Alte Fritz wäre dann
der prominenteste unter den „Sodomiten" im Bild, die deshalb dargestellt
wurden, um den Lord zu verhöhnen, der ja von seiner Frau gehörnt wird,
weil er ihre sexuellen Bedürfnisse nicht erfüllt.

---

23 Sicher nicht zufällig wurde der Name „Timothy" im damaligen englischen Sprachgebrauch für einen
Kinderpenis verwendet! Siehe James Orchard Halliwell: *A Dictionary of Archaic and Provincial Words, Ob-
solete Phrases, Proverbs, and Ancient Customs, from the Fourteenth Century,* 2 Bände, 2. Aufl. (London: John
Russell Smith 1852), Band II, 875; Joseph Wright (Hrsg.): *The English Dialect Dictionary, Being the Complete
Vocabulary of all Dialect Words Still in Use, or Known to have been in Use during the Last Two Hundred Years,*
6 Bände (London: Henry Frowde 1898–1905), Band VI, 153.

Simon François Ravenet nach William Hogarth: *Marriage A-la-Mode*, Plate 4 (1745).

Den meisten Raum in Hogarths Bild aber beansprucht, auch körperlich, die wohlbeleibte Gestalt des Sängers ganz vorne: ein mit weiblichem Schmuck üppig ausgestatteter Kastrat. Man beachte die vielen mit Brillanten besetzten Ringe am Ohr und an den Fingern. Bei diesem vom Künstler so deutlich als „Schwuchtel" gekennzeichneten Sänger mag es sich um eine Anspielung auf Senesino, Carestini oder einen der anderen italienischen Kastraten handeln, wie sie Händel, dem einige Experten Kontakte zu homosexuellen Kreisen nachsagen,[24] in den 1730er Jahren für seine italienischen

---

24 Siehe etwa Ellen T. Harris: *Handel as Orpheus: Voice and Desire in the Chamber Cantatas* (Cambridge, MA und London: Harvard University Press 2001); dies.: "Homosexual Context and Identity: Reflections on the Reception of Handel as Orpheus", in: Chris Mounsey/Caroline Gonda (Hrsg.): *Queer People: Negotiations and Expressions of Homosexuality, 1700–1800* (Cranbury, NJ: Associated University Presses 2007), 41–66; Gary C. Thomas: " 'Was George Frideric Handel Gay?' On Closet Questions and Cultural Politics", in: Philip Brett/Elizabeth Wood/Gary C. Thomas (Hrsg.): *Queering the Pitch: The New Gay and Lesbian Musicology*, 2. Aufl. (New York und Abingdon: Routledge 2006), 155–203. Ein strikter Gegner einer solchen Ansicht ist allerdings Thomas McGeary: "Handel and Homosexuality: Burlington House and Cannons Revisited", *Journal of the Royal Musical Association* 136, Nr. 1 (Mai 2011), 33–71.

Opern in London engagiert hatte.[25] Oder könnte es sich bei dem Sänger gar um eine Anspielung auf Georg Friedrich Händel selber handeln?

Balthasar Denner: *Georg Friedrich Händel* (ca. 1726–28)

Joseph Goupy: *The Charming Brute* (1754)

Zur Entstehungszeit von Hogarths Gemälde war Händel fast pleite, weil seine italienischen Opern gescheitert waren und auch seine englischen Oratorien in London zunächst wenig Erfolg hatten,[26] weshalb der Künstler den

---

25 Siehe zu den in Frage kommenden Kastraten: *Handel and the Castrati: The Story Behind the 18th Century Superstar Singers*, Aust.-Kat., Handel House Museum, London, 29. März–1. Oktober 2006; Alan Riding: "In Opera, a Different Kind of Less Is More: 'Handel and the Castrati' ", *New York Times*, 19. April 2006, wo Francesco Bernardi (besser bekannt als Senesino), Giovanni Carestini, der so gut wie Farinelli singen konnte, Gioacchino Conti, der unter dem Künstlernamen Gizziello auftrat, und Gaetano Majorano, genannt Caffarelli, unter den von Händel engagierten Kastraten erwähnt werden. Jeremy Barlow macht allerdings darauf aufmerksam, dass die drei Kastraten, die von den Interpreten am häufigsten genannt werden, wenn es um die Identifizierung des Sängers in Hogarths Bild geht, England lange verlassen hatten, bevor es zur Ausführung der *Marriage A-la-Mode*-Bilder kam: „Carestini was in the country in the period 1733–35, Senesino in 1720–36, and Farinelli in 1734–37. This is not necessarily an argument against their identification with the figure in the print, because we see in *The Enraged Musician* that Hogarth did not always locate his works chronologically at the time when he made them; the poster for *The Beggar's Opera* added to the final state describes the first run in 1728, yet the engraving was published in 1741 (...)." Siehe Jeremy Barlow: *'The Enraged Musician': Hogarth's Musical Imagery* (Aldershot, Hampshire: Ashgate Publishing Limited 2005), 194.

26 Am 17. Januar 1745 beklagte der Komponist selber im *Daily Advertiser* den „Loss of the publick Favour". Näheres zu Händels Misserfolgen in jenen Tagen, die sich schon ein Jahr zuvor abzuzeichnen begannen, bei William Barclay Squire: "Handel in 1745", in: Carl Mennicke (Hrsg.): *Riemann-Festschrift: Gesammelte Studien, Hugo Riemann zum sechzigsten Geburtstage überreicht von Freunden und Schülern* (Leipzig: Max Hesse 1909), 423–433; William C. Smith: "Handel's Failure in 1745: New Letters", in: *Concerning Handel: His Life and Works. Essays by William C. Smith* (London: Cassell & Co. 1948), 145–161.

William Hogarth: *Marriage A-la-Mode*, Bild 4. Gemälde (1743/44; National Gallery, London). Detail.

Komponisten ironisch als einen Sänger dargestellt haben könnte, der sich mit Engagements in kleinen privaten Zirkeln durchschlagen musste.[27]

---

27 Einige Händel-Porträts, so das Gemälde von Balthasar Denner (ca. 1726–28, National Portrait Gallery, London) oder die stämmigen Beine und der Schweinerüssel in Joseph Goupys Händel-Karikatur von 1754 könnten für eine solche Hypothese sprechen. Vgl. zu diesem Blatt und verwandten früheren Händel-Karikaturen von Goupy: Ilias Chrissochoidis: "Handel, Hogarth, Goupy: artistic intersections in early Georgian England", *Early Music* 37, Nr. 4 (2009), 577–596. Es wurde ja auch vermutet, dass Handel bereits in der zweiten Szene von Hogarths *A Rake's Progress* (1735) am Cembalo sitzt. Allerdings passt die Perücke, die Hogarths Kastrat trägt, nicht zur Allonge-Perücke, wie sie auf den üblichen Händel-Porträts dargestellt ist. Auf der anderen Seite wurde behauptet, dass Händel bereits gesungen hat, noch bevor er sprechen konnte. Vgl. Sir John Hawkins: *A General History of the Science and Practice of Music*, 5 Bände

Und dieser Sänger wird von einem so berühmten Mann wie Friedrich II. auf der Querflöte begleitet? Bisher nahmen manche Interpreten an, dass es sich bei dem Musiker um Karl Friedrich Weidemann, einen Flötisten und Oboisten aus Händels Opernorchester, handeln könnte,[28] doch ist diese Mutmaßung durch nichts gerechtfertigt, zumal nicht bekannt ist, ob Weidemann homosexuell gewesen ist. Immerhin belegt diese Fehldeutung, dass es seinerzeit ein Gerücht gegeben haben muss, der von Hogarth dargestellte Flötenspieler könne ein Deutscher gewesen sein.

Auffällig ist, dass der Musiker, der im Schlafgemach der Gräfin seine Flöte erhoben hat, nicht nur mit dem Kastraten vor ihm, sondern auch mit dem *Ganymed*-Gemälde, das hinter ihm an der Wand hängt, in direkten Zusammenhang gebracht wird.[29] Weil der Adler auf diesem Bild sich seines

---

(London: Printed for T. Payne and Son 1776), Band V, 262. Tatsächlich konnte Händel fast so gut wie ein Kastrat singen: "At a concert at the house of Lady Rich, he was once prevailed on to sing a slow song, which he did in such a manner, that Farinelli, who was present, could hardly be persuaded to sing after him." Zitiert ebda., 415. Es ist ferner bekannt, dass er mit Lady Gatehouse im Duett gesungen hat. Siehe David Hunter: "Mr Handel sings Duets with Lady Gatehouse", *The Handel Institute Newsletter* 17, Nr. 1 (2006), 4–6. Aber ist es überhaupt vorstellbar, dass Hogarth den Komponisten als Sänger dargestellt haben könnte? Der Händel-Experte Donald Burrows, den ich in dieser Sache um Rat fragte, teilte mir mit: "There are not any reports or pictures of Handel singing in public. He may perhaps have sung very occasionally at private parties, though the reports are mainly about him accompanying other musicians, presumably on the harpsichord. In his *General History of the Science and Practice of Music*, Sir John Hawkins relates an anecdote about Handel singing to illustrate a point when he interviewed him." Falls Hogarth also tatsächlich eine Anspielung auf Händel als Sänger im Sinn gehabt haben sollte, dann wohl eher in Kombination mit einem Seitenhieb auf dessen „unmännliche" Kastraten.

28 Seit 1739 war Weidemann Mitglied der Royal Society of Musicians. Am 30. März 1743 und am 28. März 1744 nahm er an Benefiz-Konzerten für mittellose Musiker im Londoner King's Theatre teil. Siehe Philip H. Highfill, Jr./Kalman A. Burnim/Edward A. Langhans: *A Biographical Dictionary of Actors, Actresses, Musicians, Dancers, Managers, and Other Stage Personnel in London, 1660–1800*, Band 15: *Tibbett to M. West* (Carbondale: Southern Illinois University Press 1993), 335. Thomas Wilkes war wohl der erste, der den Flötisten als Weidemann identifizierte. Siehe Thomas Wilkes: *A General View of the Stage* (London: J. Coote und W. Whetstone 1759), 111. Ihm folgte der frühe Hogarth-Biograph John Nichols, der schrieb: „*Weideman* is playing on the *German* flute." Siehe John Nichols: *Biographical Anecdotes of William Hogarth: With a Catalogue of his Works chronologically arranged, and occasional Remarks*, 2. Aufl. (London: Printed by and for J. Nichols 1782), 223. Noch Robert Cowley, Ronald Paulson und Jeremy Barlow nennen, wenn auch mit Skepsis, den Namen des bereits in den 1720er Jahren in London nachweisbaren und 1782 verstorbenen deutschen Flötisten. Siehe Cowley: *Marriage A-la-Mode*, 108; Paulson: *Hogarth's Graphic Works*, 120; Barlow: '*The Enraged Musician*': *Hogarth's Musical Imagery*, 204–205.

29 Zum Ganymed-Mythos: Gerda Kempter: *Ganymed: Studien zur Typologie* (Köln und Wien: Böhlau 1980); Anette Kruszynski: *Der Ganymed-Mythos in Emblematik und mythographischer Literatur des 16. Jahrhunderts* (Worms: Wernersche Verlagsgesellschaft 1985); James M. Saslow: *Ganymede in the Renaissance: Homosexuality in Art and Society* (New Haven und London: Yale University Press 1986); Leonard Barkan: *Transuming Passion: Ganymede and the Erotics of Humanism* (Stanford: Stanford University Press 1991); Marcella Marongiu (Hrsg.): *Il mito di Ganimede prima e dopo Michelangelo*, Ausst.-Kat., Casa Buonarroti, 18. Juni–30. September 2002 (Florenz: Mandragora 2002); Carol Morganti: "Il mito di Ganimede nei disegni e nelle incisioni del Rinascimento", *Grafica d'arte* 16, Nr. 62 (2005), 4–15. Hogarth verwendete das Ganymed-Motiv auch an anderer Stelle in einem homoerotischen Kontext, so in seiner Ölstudie *The Marriage Contract* (ca. 1733). Siehe Ronald Paulson: *Hogarth's Harlot: Sacred Parody in Enlightenment England* (Baltimore und London: Johns Hopkins University Press 2003), 242–245. Paulson macht in diesem Zusammenhang darauf aufmerksam, dass im vulgären Sprachgebrauch der Zeit der Name "Ganymed" eine Bezeichnung für einen Knaben war, den man zur Befriedigung seiner homosexuellen Bedürfnisse

Opfers von hinten bemächtigt, dabei mit seinen Klauen die Beine Ganymeds auseinanderstemmt, um mit seinen Schwanzfedern zwischen die Schenkel des Jünglings zu fahren, handelt es sich um einen unzweideutigen Hinweis auf den von Homosexuellen praktizierten Analverkehr.[30] Zusätzlich hat Hogarth den Schnabel des Adlers so dargestellt, dass er sich in gefährlicher Weise Ganymeds Geschlechtsteil nähert, als würde dem Jüngling, wenn er sich sträuben sollte, mit einer Kastration gedroht.[31] Und ausgerechnet dieses Bild ordnet Hogarth dem Flötisten direkt zu, der auch die dazu passende „Adlernase" besitzt und ein phallisches Symbol, die Flöte, mit seinen Lippen berührt!

Nicolas Beatrizet nach Michelangelo: *Der Raub des Ganymed* (1542). Ausschnitt.

Simon François Ravenet nach William Hogarth: *Marriage A-la-Mode*, Plate 4. (1745). Ausschnitt.

War der Alte Fritz tatsächlich schwul?

Es ist bekannt, dass Friedrich der Große nicht nur exzellent Querflöte spielte, 121 Flötensonaten verfasste und mindestens viermal täglich zur Flöte gegriffen haben soll, um auf neue Gedanken zu kommen,[32] sondern auch homosexuelle Neigungen hatte und für Kastraten schwärmte. Ja, der Monarch

bezahlte oder gar missbrauchte. Siehe ebda., 243, und Thomas Blount: *Glossographia: Or a Dictionary Interpreting the Hard Words of Whatever Language, Now Used in Our Refined English Tongue*, 3. Aufl. (London: Printed by Thomas Newcomb 1670), 596.

30 Vgl. Norbert Lennartz: *"My Unwasht Muse": (De-)Konstruktionen der Erotik in der englischen Literatur des 17. Jahrhunderts* (Tübingen: Max Niemeyer Verlag 2009), 62.

31 Dieser Ansicht sind Cowley: *Marriage A-la-Mode*, 115, und Egerton: *"Zu Willliam Hogarths Zyklus Marriage A-la-Mode"*, 38. Allerdings könnte Hogarth mit seinem Motiv lediglich das sexuelle Interesse Jupiters an Ganymeds Penis betont haben.

32 Näheres über Friedrich als Flötisten bei Leonardo De Lorenzo: *My Complete Story of the Flute: The Instrument, the Performer, the Music* (Lubbock: Texas Tech University Press 1992), 78–87; Eugene E. Helms: *Music at the Court of Frederick the Great* (Norman, OK: University of Oklahoma Press 1960), Kap. II: "Frederick as Musician"; Sabine Henze-Döhring: *Friedrich der Große: Musiker und Monarch* (München: C. H. Beck 2012).

nahm die von ihm geschätzten Sänger sogar mit auf Reisen. Verzückt verkündete er seinem Freund Friedrich Graf Rothenburg: „Meine italienischen Kastraten sind im Anmarsch. Man sagt, dass sie von einem besonderen Kaliber sind und – so gut wie sie singen – ganz Berlin den Kopf verdrehen werden." Am 12. Dezember 1743 traf etwa der von ihm verpflichtete Kastrat Felice Salimbeni in der preußischen Metropole ein, der über einen Stimmumfang von zweieinhalb Oktaven verfügte und den Friedrich für den besten Sänger Italiens hielt.[33]

Es wäre nicht verwunderlich, wenn man bereits damals annahm, dass eine solche Begeisterung nur von den homoerotischen Vorlieben des Monarchen herrühren könne.[34] Schon sein Vater, Friedrich Wilhelm I., der strenge Soldatenkönig, verunglimpfte seinen verweichlichten Sohn öffentlich als „Sodomiten" und effeminierten Nichtsnutz ohne rechte männliche Inklination, der sich seine Haare wie ein Narr frisiere, mit dem Gesicht Grimassen schneide und nur für diverse Vergnügungen Interesse zeige.[35] Friedrich selbst gab als junger Kronprinz vor seinem langjährigen Vertrauten Feldmarschall Friedrich Wilhelm von Grumbkow zu, sich zu wenig vom weiblichen Geschlecht angezogen zu fühlen.[36] Tatsächlich begeisterte er sich mehr für attraktive Diener oder die „Langen Kerls" aus seinem Potsdamer Garderegiment. Den Kürassier-Leutnant Hans Hermann von Katte, seinen

---

33 Siehe Henze-Döhring: *Friedrich der Große: Musiker und Monarch*, 40–41.

34 Zum Thema ausführlich: Gaston Vorberg: *Der Klatsch über das Geschlechtsleben Friedrichs II. – Der Fall Jean-Jacques Rousseau* (Bonn: A. Marcus und E. Webers Verlag 1921) [*Abhandlungen aus dem Gebiete der Sexualforschung*, Band 3, Heft 6]; Werner Hegemann: " 'Die bekannte Schmähliteratur' und die sodomitischen und homosexuellen Anwandlungen Friedrichs II.", in: ders.: *Fridericus oder das Königsopfer*, neue, veränderte, erweiterte Auflage (Hellerau: Jakob Hegner 1926), 698–707; Gustaf Berthold Volz: "Friedrich der Große und seine sittlichen Ankläger", *Forschungen zur Brandenburgischen und Preußischen Geschichte* 41 (1928), 1–37; Susan W. Henderson: "Frederick the Great of Prussia: A Homophile Perspective", *Gai Saber* 1, Nr. 1 (Spring 1977), 46–54; James D. Steakley: "Sodomy in Enlightenment Prussia", *Journal of Homosexuality* 16, Nr. 1–2 (1988), 163–175; Bernd-Ulrich Hergemöller: *Mann für Mann: biographisches Lexikon* (Frankfurt am Main: Suhrkamp 2001), 248 ff.; Wolfgang Burgdorf: *Friedrich der Große: Ein biografisches Porträt* (Freiburg im Breisgau: Herder 2011), 67 ff.; Oliver Das Gupta: "300 Jahre Friedrich der Große – Der schwule Fritz", *Süddeutsche Zeitung*, 23. Januar 2012; Tilman Krause: "Das etwas andere Preußen: Die Historikerin Eva Ziebura über weniger bekannte Züge Friedrichs des Großen, die schwarze Pädagogik des Soldatenkönigs und Homosexualität in Zeiten der Aufklärung", *Welt am Sonntag*, 15. Januar 2012; Reinhard Alings: " 'Don't ask – don't tell' – War Friedrich schwul?" in: *Friederisiko: Friedrich der Große*, Ausst.-Kat., Stiftung Preußische Schlösser und Gärten Berlin-Brandenburg im Neuen Palais und Park Sanssouci, 28. April–28. Oktober 2012, 2 Bände (München: Hirmer 2012), Band I: *Die Ausstellung*, 238–247; Thomas Biskup: "Der kinderlose 'roi philosophe'. Herrschertugend und Sexualmoral", in: Bernd Sösemann/Gregor Vogt-Spira (Hrsg.): *Friedrich der Große in Europa: Geschichte einer wechselvollen Beziehung*, 2 Bände (Stuttgart: Franz Steiner Verlag 2012), Band I, 21–35; Ursula Pia Jauch: *Friedrichs Tafelrunde und Kants Tischgesellschaft: Ein Versuch über Preußen zwischen Eros, Philosophie und Propaganda* (Berlin: Matthes & Seitz 2014).

35 Vgl. Alings: " 'Don't ask – don't tell' – War Friedrich schwul?", 238.

36 Ebda. Zum ausgiebigen Briefwechsel zwischen Grumbkow und dem jungen Friedrich, der auf Französisch erfolgte: Reinhold Koser (Hrsg.): *Briefwechsel Friedrichs des Großen mit Grumbkow und Maupertuis (1731–1759)* (Leipzig: Verlag von S. Hirzel 1898) [*Publicationen aus den K. Preußischen Staatsarchiven*, 72].

Jugendfreund, mit dem er durchbrennen wollte, hatte Friedrichs Vater hinrichten lassen, um ein Exempel gegen die „sodomitischen" Anwandlungen seines Sohnes zu statuieren[37] – sicher ein höchst traumatisches Erlebnis für einen jungen Menschen, der sich seiner homosexuellen Neigungen sehr bewusst war. Peter Karl Christoph von Keith, der Leibpage des Kronprinzen, gehörte in jungen Jahren ebenfalls zu Friedrichs „intimem Verkehr und zu den Theilnehmern an seinen Ausschweifungen".[38] Zu seinem Kammerdiener und „Mädchen für alles" Michael Gabriel Fredersdorf unterhielt der Preußenkönig eine langjährige intime Beziehung.[39] Und es gab Eifersuchtsdramen mit seinem offen homosexuell lebenden Bruder Heinrich um die Gunst männlicher Liebhaber.[40] Über einen von beiden Brüdern gleichermaßen angehimmelten Pagen schrieb Friedrich, dass man „ihn lieben muß, wenn man ihn sieht, und anbeten, wenn man ihn kennt".[41] Einige delikate Briefe, die sich über solche Liebschaften auslassen, sollen noch unveröffentlicht im Geheimen Staatsarchiv zu Berlin schlummern.[42]

Kein Wunder, dass Johann Georg Hamann den Preußenkönig als „Aftokrator" beschimpfte und die Männer in seinem Umkreis „warme Brüder" nannte.[43] Voltaire, der mit als erster die Homosexualität des Monarchen öffentlich machte, pflegte Friedrich *Luc* zu nennen. Rückwärts gelesen,

37 Siehe neben den Standard-Biographien über Friedrich den Großen auch Hergemöller: *Mann für Mann*, 411–412; Detlef Merten: *Der Katte-Prozeß: Vortrag gehalten vor der Berliner Juristischen Gesellschaft am 14. Februar 1979* (Berlin: Walter de Gruyter 1980) [*Schriftenreihe der Juristischen Gesellschaft zu Berlin*, 62].

38 Bernhard von Poten: "Keith, Peter Karl Christof", in: *Allgemeine Deutsche Biographie*, Band 15 (Leipzig: Duncker & Humblot 1882), 555.

39 Siehe Alings: " 'Don't ask – don't tell' – War Friedrich schwul?", 239, 242, 243; Johannes Richter (Hrsg.): *Die Briefe Friedrichs des Großen an seinen vormaligen Kammerdiener Fredersdorf* (Berlin: Hermann Klemm 1926); Klaus Bustrin: " 'Ich habe gemeinet, du häst mihr lieb': Friedrichs enge Beziehungen zu seinem Kammerdiener Fredersdorf", *Potsdamer Neueste Nachrichten*, 1. September 2012.

40 Siehe Gerd Fesser: "Der König von Rheinsberg: Ein Preuße für heute: Genialisch, kunstsinnig, europäisch und ein bisschen schwul – Prinz Heinrich, Bruder Friedrichs II., wird jetzt in Brandenburg gefeiert", *Die Zeit*, Nr. 32 (1. August 2002). Näheres zur Homosexualität von Friedrichs Bruder bei Numa Praetorius [= Eugen Wilhelm]: "Die Homosexualität des Prinzen Heinrich, des Bruders Friedrichs des Großen", *Zeitschrift für Sexualwissenschaft* 15 (1929), 465–476; Eva Ziebura: *Prinz Heinrich von Preußen* (Berlin: Stapp Verlag 1999); Burkhardt Göres/Claudia Sommer/Detlef Fuchs: *Prinz Heinrich von Preußen: Ein Europäer in Rheinsberg*, Ausst.-Kat., Schloss Rheinsberg, 4. August–27. Oktober 2002 (München und Berlin: Deutscher Kunstverlag 2002).

41 Zitiert bei Ziebura: *Prinz Heinrich von Preußen*, 46.

42 Siehe Alings: " 'Don't ask – don't tell' – War Friedrich schwul?", 242.

43 Siehe Johann Georg Hamann: "Des Ritters von Rosencreuz letzte Willensmeinung über den göttlichen und menschlichen Ursprung der Sprache: Aus einer Caricaturbilderurschrift eilfertig übersetzt vom Handlanger des Hierophanten" [1772], in: Friedrich Roth (Hrsg.): *Hamann's Schriften*, Vierter Theil (Berlin: bey G. Reimer 1823), 28. Vgl. auch Paul Derks: *Die Schande der heiligen Päderastie: Homosexualität und Öffentlichkeit in der deutschen Literatur 1750 bis 1850* (Berlin: Verlag Rosa Winkel 1990), 90–91; Wolfgang Müller: "Seid reinlich bei Tage und säuisch bei Nacht (Goethe) oder: Betrachtungen über die schönste Sache der Welt im Spiegel der deutschen Sprache – einst und jetzt", in: Rudolf Hoberg (Hrsg.): *Sprache – Erotik – Sexualität* (Berlin: Erich Schmidt Verlag 2001), 26.

heißt es *cul* (französisch „Hintern").[44] Er beschrieb das Liebesleben des Königs wie folgt:

> „War seine Majestät gekleidet und gestiefelt, huldigte der Stoiker für ein paar Augenblicke der Sekte Epikurs: er ließ zwei oder drei Favoriten kommen, Leutnants aus seinem Regiment oder Pagen, Heiduken oder junge Kadetten. Man trank Kaffee. Derjenige, der das Taschentuch zugeworfen bekam, blieb eine halbe Stunde mit dem König allein. Es kam dabei nicht bis zum Äußersten, da der Prinz zu Lebzeiten seines Vaters bei seinen flüchtigen Liebschaften ziemlich malträtiert und schlecht geheilt worden war; die erste Rolle konnte er nicht spielen, er mußte sich mit der zweiten begnügen."[45]

Ähnlich berichtet der Baron von Diebitsch, dass Seine Majestät „verschiedene Ihrer Lieblinge" sowohl nachmittags als auch morgens an der besagten Kaffeetafel teilnehmen ließ, unter ihnen auch ein Page namens von Sydow.[46]

Zum eher passiven Part, den der schmächtige Friedrich laut Voltaire bei der gleichgeschlechtlichen Liebe spielte, äußert sich auch Casanova in seinen Memoiren. Wir lesen dort, dass die Soldaten des ersten Potsdamer Bataillons „alle in den Uhrtäschchen ihrer Hosen eine goldene Uhr hatten. So belohnte der König den Mut, den sie bewiesen, als sie ihn unters Joch nahmen [...] Man machte gar keinen Hehl daraus."[47]

---

44 Siehe Das Gupta: "300 Jahre Friedrich der Große – Der schwule Fritz"; J[ohann] D. E. Preuß: *Friedrich der Große: Eine Lebensgeschichte*, Band I (Berlin: In der Nauckschen Buchhandlung 1832), 365.

45 Zitiert bei Bringmann: *Friedrich der Große*, 74. Zu diesem und weiteren Zitaten: Voltaire: *Über den König von Preußen: Memoiren*, hrsg. und übersetzt von Anneliese Botond (Frankfurt am Main: Insel Verlag 1967). Vgl. über Friedrich den Großen und Voltaire auch Louis Crompton: *Homosexuality & Civilization* (Cambridge, MA und London: Belknap Press of Harvard University Press 2003), 504–518.

46 Siehe Carl Friedrich-Wilhelm von Diebitsch: *Specielle Zeit- und Geschäfts-Eintheilung König Friedrich des Zweyten* (St. Petersburg: mit Bewilligung der Censur, gedruckt in der Schnoorschen Buchdruckerey 1802), 27. Allerdings betont von Diebitsch auch: „Fast durchgehends wurde die Gnade Sr Majestät", welche „verschiedenen solchen Männern aus allerley Ständen erwiesen" worden war, „mit Undankbarkeit belohnt [...]" Über den Pagen von Sydow schreibt K. F. Reiche, dass er am 28. Juli 1746 zu seinem Geburtstag vom König eine Uniform geschenkt bekam und vor den Augen Friedrichs sein Pagenkleid ausziehen musste, um diese anzuprobieren. In der linken Uniformtasche fand der junge Mann einen Zettel vor, auf dem stand, dass Seine Königliche Majestät „den Pagen v. Sydow wegen seiner [...] artigen und niedlichen Leichtfertigkeiten, wie auch wegen der großen Qualität, einen guten Kaffee mit Ziegenmilch zu trinken, zum Lieutenant und Flügel-Adjutanten" ernannt hätte und er im königlichen Hause „bei allen durchtriebenen Leichtfertigkeiten mit der Aussprache eines deutschen R." sein Bestes zu geben habe. Im Anhang fügt der Autor hinzu, dass von Sydow von Friedrich „wahrhaft väterlich behandelt" worden sei, ja dass er „ein Werkzeug der angeblichen griechischen Liebe des Königs gewesen" ist. Siehe K. F. Reiche: *Friedrich der Große und seine Zeit: Nach den besten Quellen dargestellt* (Leipzig: Christian Ernst Kollmann 1840), 177–178, 536.

47 Giacomo Casanova, Chevalier de Seingalt: *Geschichte meines Lebens*, hrsg. von Erich Loos, übersetzt von Heinz von Sauter, 12 Bände (Berlin: Propyläen Verlag 1964–1967), Band X, 87.

Selbst die Sammelleidenschaft des kunstliebenden Monarchen blieb nicht unbeeinflusst von seinen homosexuellen Vorlieben. So wurde 1747 die berühmte antike Bronzestatue des *Betenden Knaben*, den man früher für eine Darstellung des Antinous hielt, von Friedrich wohl vor allem wegen ihrer erotischen Wirkung erworben und in Sanssouci aufgestellt.[48] Ferner berichtet der bekannte Berliner Aufklärer und Chronist Friedrich Nicolai, dass der König über den Kunsthändler Jacques Trible eine von Giulio Romano in Tusche gezeichnete „Priapeje" erworben hat.[49]

Durch Nicolai ist ebenfalls überliefert, dass Friedrich mit Hilfe von eigens angefertigten „unzüchtigen" Gemälden allerlei Schabernack mit Gästen im Potsdamer Schloss trieb. Als der König z. B. hörte, dass der alte Herzog von Hollstein-Beck „weiblichen Besuch" bestellt hatte, ließ er geschwind einen „ganz ordinären Maler ein kleines, nicht völlig einen Fuß hohes Gemälde, einen Satyr mit einer Nymphe malen, mit einem grünen Vorhang davor, und es unvermerkt in das Zimmer des Herzogs hängen." Als ein anderes Mal der „Fürst Bischof von Breßlau bey einem Besuche in eben dem Zimmer logirte, ließ der König auf eben die Art das Gemälde eines Mönchs und einer Nonne malen, und auch in das Zimmer hängen."[50] Selbst während seiner Tafelrunden, an denen auch Friedrichs enger Freund Francesco Alga-

---

48 Siehe Thomas Fischbacher: *Des Königs Knabe: Friedrich der Große und Antinous* (Weimar: VDG 2011).

49 Hofrat Jacques Trible war ein Berliner Kunsthändler, den Friedrich öfter für seine Besorgung von "tableaux" entlohnte, wie aus den "Schatullrechnungen" des Königs hervorgeht. Siehe Nina Simone Schepkowski: *Johann Ernst Gotzkowsky: Kunstagent und Gemäldesammler im friderizianischen Berlin* (Berlin: Akademie Verlag 2009), 121n426, 150, 249, 375, 427, 428, 429. Nicolai schreibt: „Kommerzienrath Trible, ein Mann, der sehr viele Gemälde an den König verkauft hat, und ein wahrer Kenner der Kunst war, besaß eine ganz vortreffliche Zeichnung in Tusch von Giulio Romano, eine Priapeje, die er dem Könige anbot. Der König konnte sich lange nicht entschließen; endlich kaufte er sie doch, und bezahlte sie sehr gut, weil es eine der herrlichsten, ausgeführtesten und wohlkonservirtesten Zeichnungen dieses Meisters war. Und der König damals sich ernstlich befliß, die verschiedenen Manieren der Maler zu studiren." Doch fühlt sich der Autor verpflichtet, mit moralischem Unterton zu ergänzen, dass dieses Blatt wegen der allzu erotischen Motive nicht lange im Besitz Friedrichs verblieb: „Nachdem er aber diese Zeichnung eine kurze Zeit gehabt hatte, verschenkte er sie, weil ihm der Gegenstand allzusehr zuwider war." Siehe Friedrich Nicolai (Hrsg.): *Anekdoten von König Friedrich II. von Preussen, und von einigen Personen, die um Ihn waren*, Fünftes Heft (Berlin und Stettin 1791), 107–108. Schließlich durfte ein preußischer König – zumindest offiziell – nicht zu sehr für unmoralische Kunst schwärmen, weshalb sich Nicolai in seiner Schrift auch groß und breit gegen die von anderer Seite geäußerte Behauptung wehrt, in Friedrichs Räumen hätten unzüchtige Gemälde gehangen. Möglicherweise handelte es sich bei der erwähnten Zeichnung um eine Vorstudie zu Giulio Romanos *Faune und Bacchanten bringen Priapus ein Opfer* oder aber um eine bewusste Fälschung, wie sie im 18. Jahrhundert gar nicht selten war. In letzterem Falle hätte die Tuschzeichnung wohl spezielle erotische Motive dem Stich entlehnt, den der sog. „Meister B mit dem Würfel" nach Giulio Romanos Originalzeichnung angefertigt hat. Siehe J. D. Passavant: *Rafael von Urbino und sein Vater Giovanni Santi*, Zweiter Theil (Leipzig: F. A. Brockhaus 1839), 656; Stefania Massari: *Giulio Romano pinxit et delineavit: Opere grafiche autografe di collaborazione e bottega*, Ausst.-Kat., Palazzo della Farnesina, Rom, 11. Februar–10. April 1993 (Rom: Fratelli Palombi 1993), Nr. 50.

50 Und Nicolai betont: „[...] beide Gemälde sind noch vorhanden. Ich habe [...] sie in der Beschreibung von Potsdam deswegen nicht angeben wollen, weil sie gar keinen malerischen Werth haben [...]." Siehe Nicolai: *Anekdoten von König Friedrich II. von Preussen*, Fünftes Heft, 95–96.

rotti teilnahm[51] und bei denen es meist zwanglos-fröhlich und ohne festgeschriebene Etikette zuging,[52] ist der Monarch – vor allem, wenn (wie so oft) keine Frauen zugegen waren – zweideutigen Erzählungen gegenüber sehr aufgeschlossen gewesen. So berichtet sein Arzt Johann Georg von Zimmermann, dass Friedrich mehr als einmal eine schlüpfrige Geschichte über den an starkem Fieber erkrankten Kaiser Leopold zum Besten gab: Auf Anordnung seines Leibarztes sei der Kaiser in einen hermetisch abgeschlossenen und gänzlich abgedunkelten Raum gebracht worden. Doch hatte der Doktor Probleme, das Bett des Monarchen im stockfinsteren Zimmer zu finden.

> „Endlich gelangs. Aber nun war der Herr Leibarzt in grosser Noth, wie und wo er, den Arm des Kaisers finden solle, um den Puls zu fühlen. Er betastete, sehr bedächtlich, die Bettdecke, das Bett, und den Kaiser: mit dem sichs jetzt nicht sprechen ließ, denn er war ein sehr gravitätischer Mann. Endlich gelang auch dieß; und der Herr Leibarzt glaubte: nun habe er den Arm des Kaisers! – Er zählte also, höchst aufmerksam, und mit zusammengekniffenem Gesichte, die Pulse. Aber der Kaiser, über diesen unverschämten Mißgriff erstaunt, brachte mit der höchsten Würde, den dummen Leibarzt aus seinem Irrthum, indem Er pathetisch, bedächtlich und langsam, zu diesem Esculap sagte: hoc est membrum nostrum imperiale sacro-caesareum."[53]

Solche deftig-zotigen Scherze deuten darauf hin, dass Friedrich II. nicht prüde war und seinen speziellen sexuellen Gelüsten gegenüber recht aufgeschlossen gewesen sein dürfte, ja man ist geneigt anzunehmen, dass er sie relativ offen auslebte und nicht, wie von manchen Historikern gerne behauptet wird, zugunsten eines asexuellen Lebens unterdrückt hat.[54] Kein

---

51 Graf Algarotti, der so alt wie Friedrich war, ja mit diesem über die Freuden des Orgasmus korrespondierte, hatte bereits in London dem homosexuellen Zirkel um Lord Hervey angehört, der auch von Hogarth porträtiert wurde. Vgl. Norbert Schmitz: *Der italienische Freund: Francesco Algarotti und Friedrich der Große* (Hannover: Wehrhahn Verlag 2012); Ursula Pia Jauch: "Eros zwischen Herr und Knecht: Friedrich der Grosse und Francesco Algarotti im Land der Lust", in: Bernd Sösemann (Hrsg.): *Friedrich der Grosse in Europa – gefeiert und umstritten* (Stuttgart: Franz Steiner Verlag 2012), 59–70.

52 Hierzu ausführlicher: Ursula Pia Jauch: "Annotationen zu den Asylanten, Querdenkern und Avantgardisten in der 'Tafelrunde', oder: Die Gemeinschaft der Epikureer zu Sanssouci", in: Bernd Sösemann/Gregor Vogt-Spira (Hrsg.): *Friedrich der Grosse in Europa: Geschichte einer wechselvollen Beziehung*, Band I (Stuttgart: Franz Steiner Verlag 2012), 68–111; dies.: *Friedrichs Tafelrunde und Kants Tischgesellschaft*.

53 [Johann Georg] Ritter von Zimmermann: *Fragmente über Friedrich den Grossen zur Geschichte seines Lebens, seiner Regierung, und seines Charakters*, 3 Bände (Leipzig: in der Weidmannischen Buchhandlung 1790), Band II, 260–261.

54 Noch Hans-Joachim Neumann schließt eine „reaktive (weitestgehende) Asexualität" bei Friedrich nicht aus. Siehe Neumann: *Friedrich der Große: Feldherr und Philosoph*, 51–52. Auch die Annahme, Friedrich hätte die Homosexualität nur als „Mode des achtzehnten Jahrhunderts" mitgemacht, entbehrt jeder

Wunder, dass auch der bekanntermaßen homosexuelle Klassizist Johann Joachim Winckelmann wegen des „griechischen Geschmacks in der Liebe",
der an Friedrichs Hof herrschte, voll auf seine Kosten kam. In einem Brief
vom 27. März 1752 an seinen Freund Hieronymus Dietrich Berendis schrieb
er voller Begeisterung über seinen Besuch in Sanssouci: „Ich habe Wollüste
genoßen, die ich nicht wieder genieße werde: ich habe Athen und Sparta in
Potsdam gesehen und bin mit einer anbetungsvollen Verehrung gegen den
göttlichen Monarchen erfüllet."[55]

Jedenfalls kann kein Zweifel darüber bestehen, dass schon Mitte des
18. Jahrhunderts erstaunlich viele Zeitgenossen mit großer Selbstverständ-
lichkeit dem Preußenkönig homosexuelle Neigungen unterstellten,[56] auch
wenn es den heute für die gleichgeschlechtliche Liebe verwendeten Be-
griff damals noch nicht gab. Zwar versucht Zimmermann, in seinen *Frag-
menten über Friedrich den Grossen* in einem eigens verfassten Kapitel „Ueber
Friedrichs vorgeblich griechischen Geschmack in der Liebe"[57] die Ehre des
Monarchen dadurch zu retten, dass er behauptet, der Kronprinz hätte vor
seiner Scheinehe mit Elisabeth Christine von Braunschweig-Wolfenbüttel
keine Abneigung gegenüber Frauenzimmern gehabt, ja sich beim „kurzen
und geraden Umgang mit Freudenmädchen" kurz vor der Hochzeit eine
Geschlechtskrankheit zugezogen. Um den „äussert heftigen venerischen
Samenfluß" zu stoppen, hätte er sich in die Hände eines Quacksalbers bege-
ben, der ihn falsch behandelt habe, so dass er ein halbes Jahr später in eine
derart „heftige Krankheit" verfiel, die nur ein „grausamer Schnitt" zu kurie-
ren vermochte. Dieser allerdings hätte den Monarchen so verstümmelt, dass
er sich für zeugungsunfähig hielt und sich nicht mehr traute, sich vor anderen zu entblößen und mit seiner Frau zu schlafen.[58] Für Oliver Das Gupta
ist das Kalkül von Zimmermanns erfundener Story klar: „Ein teutonischer
Held hatte weder asexuell, noch homosexuell zu sein – aber ein ‚galantes
Leiden' billigte man einem solchen Idol zu." So dürfte seiner Ansicht nach
Wolfgang Burgdorf richtig liegen, der meint: „Friedrich hatte einen körper-
lichen Ekel vor Frauen, er war unfähig, mit ihnen zu schlafen."[59] Vor allem

---

Grundlage. Siehe zu solchen Rechtfertigungsversuchen: Hegemann: " ‚Die bekannte Schmähliteratur'
und die sodomitischen und homosexuellen Anwandlungen Friedrichs II.", 707.

55 Zitiert bei Martin Disselkamp: *Die Stadt der Gelehrten: Studien zu Johann Joachim Winckelmanns Briefen aus Rom* (Tübingen: Max Niemeyer Verlag 1993), 151n104.

56 Siehe auch Bringmann: *Friedrich der Große*, 68.

57 Von Zimmermann: *Fragmente über Friedrich den Grossen zur Geschichte seines Lebens, seiner Regierung,
und seines Charakters*, Band I, 63–90.

58 Ebda., 66–73.

59 Siehe Das Gupta: "300 Jahre Friedrich der Große – Der schwule Fritz".

sind ja auch die vielen zeitgenössischen Stimmen nicht wegzudiskutieren, die selbst Zimmermann freimütig zitiert:

> „Der berlinische Oberconsistorialrath, Herr Büsching, sagt: ‚Durch seinen Widerwillen gegen das Frauenzimmer verlohr Friedrich viel sinnliches Vergnügen. Aber er verschaffte sichs wieder durch den Umgang mit Mannspersonen; und hatte aus der Geschichte der Philosophie behalten daß man dem Socrates nachgesagt, er habe den Umgang mit dem Alcibiades geliebt.' Aber nicht nur Herr Büsching, sondern Voltaire, la Beaumelle, der Herzog von Choiseul, unzählige Franzosen und Deutsche, fast alle Freunde und Feinde Friedrichs, fast alle Fürsten und Grossen in Europa, sogar seine Bedienten, sogar die Vertrauten und Gesellschafter seiner letzten Jahre glaubten: Friedrich habe geliebt, wie man sagt, daß Socrates den Alcibiades liebte."[60]

Deutliche Worte! Der König selbst war der Verfasser des komischen, frivol-blasphemischen Heldengedichts *Le Palladion* (1749), das mit Anspielungen unterhalb der Gürtellinie nicht spart und in dem homosexuelle Aktivitäten als etwas Selbstverständliches beschrieben werden. Darin findet sich nicht nur eine Aufzählung berühmter Homosexueller von Alkibiades bis Caesar, sondern auch folgende gotteslästerliche Strophe:

> „Was meinst du wohl, das Johannes machte,
> Damit er Jesus stets zur Seiten lag?
> Er machte seinen lieben Ganymed."[61]

Insofern passt der Flöte spielende Preußenkönig recht gut zum *Ganymed*-Gemälde und zu den anderen Homosexuellen in Hogarths Bild – darunter auch ein Mann, der weiter hinten „winke, winke" macht und an dessen Handgelenk ein Fächer baumelt.

Dass der Ganymed-Mythos ganz nach dem Geschmack des Monarchen gewesen zu sein scheint, erweist sich auch daran, dass auf dem 1768 fertig-

---

60 Zimmermann: *Fragmente über Friedrich den Grossen zur Geschichte seines Lebens, seiner Regierung, und seines Charakters*, Band I, 63–64. Hierzu auch Crompton: *Homosexuality & Civilization*, 505–506. Sokrates war der jugendlichen Schönheit des athenischen Staatsmanns und Feldherrn Alkibiades verfallen und soll ein intimes Verhältnis zu ihm gehabt haben – ob rein platonisch oder auch sexuell, ist umstritten.

61 H. D. Kittsteiner: *Das Komma von Sans, Souci: Ein Forschungsbericht mit Fußnoten* (Heidelberg: Manutius Verlag 2001), 45. Interessant ist, dass der *Moralisierte Ovid* aus dem 14. Jahrhundert Ganymed ernsthaft als Vorwegnahme des Evangelisten Johannes interpretiert hat. Siehe Erwin Panofsky: "Die neoplatonische Bewegung und Michelangelo", in: ders.: *Studien zur Ikonologie: Humanistische Themen in der Kunst der Renaissance* (Köln: DuMont Buchverlag 1980), 279. Ob der belesene Friedrich davon wusste?

gestellten Deckengemälde für den Marmorsaal des Potsdamer Neuen Palais dargestellt ist, wie Ganymed in den Olymp eingeführt und durch Hebe, die Göttin der Jugend, zu Jupiters Göttertafel geleitet wird. Doch als der König das von Charles-Amédée Philippe van Loo gemalte Werk näher in Augenschein nahm, entdeckte er auf einer Tafel, die von Genien des Ruhmes hinter Jupiter herangetragen wird, seine Initialen. Entrüstet befahl er die Entfernung der Buchstaben.[62] War es ihm etwa peinlich, dass sein Name mit Ganymed in direkten Zusammenhang gebracht wurde? Und lag dies etwa daran, dass Friedrich die 1745 erschienene Stichversion von Hogarths *Marriage A-la-Mode* kannte und sich in dem Flötenspieler vor dem *Ganymed*-Bild wiedererkannt hat?

Woher kannte Hogarth die Adlernase des Alten Fritz?

Über die sexuellen Vorlieben des preußischen Monarchen wusste Hogarth offenbar bestens Bescheid. Wie aber konnte er zur Entstehungszeit seines Bildes, also 1743/44, darüber informiert gewesen sein, dass der Alte Fritz eine gebogene Nase hatte, wie die Totenmaske des Monarchen eindrucksvoll demonstriert?

Über die seinerzeit verbreiteten Porträts sicher nicht. Vielleicht über britische Adlige oder Leute aus dem Umfeld Voltaires, von denen einige Friedrich persönlich begegnet sind? Nicht nur über diese Kanäle: Der Künstler hatte während seines Parisaufenthaltes im Mai und Juni 1743[63] tatsächlich

---

62 „In dem großen Marmorsaale im oberen Geschosse des neuen Schlosses bey Sanssouci malte Vanloo, auf Befehl des Königs, zum Deckenstücke eine Versammlung der Götter. Dieser Maler ließ sich einfallen, ein paar Famen [= Genien der Ruhmverkündigung] vorzustellen, welche den Namenszug des Königs mit Lorbern umkränzt den versammleten Göttern darbringen. Der König besah dieses Deckenstück nicht eher als bis der Saal schon beynahe fertig war. Dem Könige gefiel überhaupt das Gemälde wegen der Härte des Kolorits nicht; als er aber seinen Namenszug erblickte, ward er äußerst entrüstet. Er befahl, daß augenblicklich alles sich dahin beziehende sollte ausgelöscht werden. Es mußte dazu abermals ein besonderes Gerüste aufgebauet werden, das mit allen Umständen ein paar hundert Thaler kostete. Vanloo konnte sich nicht anders helfen, als eine grüne Decke über den Namenszug zu malen, denn die ganzen Figuren der Famen konnte er nicht auslöschen. Wer dieses Deckenstück betrachtet, und die Umstände nicht weiß, wird nicht begreifen können, warum die Famen den Göttern etwas verdecktes darbringen. Es ist ein Denkmal der Bescheidenheit Friedrichs des Großen." Friedrich Nicolai (Hrsg.): *Anekdoten von König Friedrich II. von Preussen, und von einigen Personen, die um Ihn waren*, Drittes Heft (Berlin und Stettin 1789), 281–282. Siehe auch Franziska Windt: „Künstlerische Inszenierung von Größe: Friedrichs Selbstdarstellung im Neuen Palais", in: *Friederisiko: Friedrich der Große*, Ausst.-Kat., Stiftung Preußische Schlösser und Gärten Berlin-Brandenburg im Neuen Palais und Park Sanssouci, 28. April–28. Oktober 2012, 2 Bände (München: Hirmer 2012), Band II: *Die Essays*, 130–149; Gerd Bartoschek: *Die Gemälde im Neuen Palais* (Potsdam-Sanssouci: Generaldirektion der Staatlichen Schlösser und Gärten 1976), 3, 6n4 und 28, Nr. 199.

63 Zu diesem Paris-Aufenthalt ausführlich: Robin Simon: „Un rosbif à Paris: Hogarth's visit to Paris in 1743", *The British Art Journal* 7, Nr. 2 (Autumn 2006), 24–33; ders.: *Hogarth, France and British Art: The rise of the arts in eighteenth-century Britain* (London: Hogarth Arts, Distributed by Paul Holberton Publishing 2007), Kap. 2. Simon vermutet, dass Hogarth das erste Gemälde der *Marriage A-la-Mode*-Serie mit nach Paris nahm, um dort „the most blasé of French engravers" für sein Projekt zu begeistern, die sechsteilige Bilderserie im französischen Stil nachstechen zu lassen. Zudem glaubt Simon, erhebliche Differenzen zwischen den kühleren Tönen auf der Leinwand des ersten Gemäldes und den wärmeren Tönen der nach-

 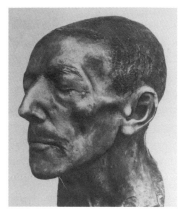

Simon François Ravenet nach William Hogarth: *Marriage A-la-Mode*, Plate 4 (1745). Ausschnitt.

Totenmaske Friedrichs des Großen (1786)

die Gelegenheit, sich ganz konkret über das Aussehen des Preußenkönigs zu informieren. Auf der Suche nach französischen Kupferstechern für die geplante Stichversion von *Marriage A-la-Mode,* die ihn in die Ateliers zahlreicher Künstler der Académie Royale führte,[64] dürfte Hogarth auch auf Georg Friedrich Schmidt (1712–1775) gestoßen sein, der sich damals in der französischen Metropole wegen seiner weichen und feinen Linienführung den Ruf eines herausragenden Stechers erworben hatte und 1743 an einem Porträt Friedrichs den Großen arbeitete.[65]

Dieser deutsche Kupferstecher und Radierer war zunächst in Berlin ausgebildet worden, wo er mit dem Hofmaler Antoine Pesne Freundschaft schloss, der seit 1711 am preußischen Hof tätig war und „in intimem, persönlichem Verkehr" mit Friedrich dem Großen stand.[66] In Berlin hatte Schmidt auch schon Bildnisse des gleichaltrigen jungen Kronprinzen gesto-

---

folgenden Bilder zu erkennen, die nur dadurch zu erklären seien, dass der Künstler die erste Szene vor seiner Reise nach Paris gemalt, die anderen Ölbilder jedoch – unter dem Eindruck französischer Kunst – erst nach seiner Rückkehr nach England fertiggestellt hat.

64 Bereits Hogarths englischer Künstlerkollege Joseph Highmore hatte bei seinem Parisaufenthalt 1734 viele französische Künstler in ihren Ateliers, aber auch in der Académie Royale und in ihren Privatwohnungen besucht. Es ist anzunehmen, dass Hogarth dasselbe tat. Simon denkt, dass er Jean Baptiste Siméon Chardin und Maurice Quentin de La Tour sowie zahlreiche weitere Künstler aus ihrem Umkreis getroffen hat, denn einige Motive in seinen Werken deuten auf Einflüsse dieser Maler hin. Vgl. Simon: "Un rosbif à Paris: Hogarth's visit to Paris in 1743", 24–25, 30.

65 Siehe J. E. Wessely: *Georg Friedrich Schmidt: Verzeichniss seiner Stiche und Radirungen* (Hamburg: Haendcke & Lehmkuhl 1887), 18, Nr. 41; *Fridericus-Stiche: Eine Hommage an Friedrich den Grossen,* 24. Einen Besuch bei Schmidt erwähnt Robin Simon zwar nicht, aber weil der deutsche Künstler bereits damals „allgemein als einer der besten Kupferstecher von Paris" galt, dürfte ihn Hogarth nicht übersehen haben, zumal Schmidt eng mit La Tour befreundet war und die französische Manier gut beherrschte. Siehe Wessely: *Georg Friedrich Schmidt: Verzeichniss seiner Stiche und Radirungen,* X–XI.

66 Siehe Seidel: *Friedrich der Grosse und die bildende Kunst,* 40, 151.

Georg Friedrich Schmidt. *Friedrich der Große* (1/43)

chen,[67] ging dann aber 1737 mit einem Empfehlungsschreiben Pesnes nach Paris, wo er seine Rokokomanier zur Perfektion vervollkommnete[68] und so erfolgreich war, dass er mit Sondergenehmigung des französischen Königs 1742 als Protestant zur Académie Royale zugelassen wurde.[69]

Es ist daher mehr als wahrscheinlich, dass Hogarth auch diesen aufstrebenden deutschen Kupferstecher in seine engere Wahl gezogen hat, die gra-

---

67 Ebda., 219.

68 Laut Paul Dehnert „pflegte Georg Friedrich Schmidt die Rokokokunst. Ihre Ausdrucksweise hatte er sich schon früh in Berlin angeeignet, in Paris war er mit ihr zur Meisterschaft gelangt [...]" Siehe Paul Dehnert: "Georg Friedrich Schmidt, der Hofkupferstecher des Königs", *Jahrbuch Preussischer Kulturbesitz* 16 (1979), 332.

69 Der Generalkontrolleur der Finanzen, Philibert Orry, schickte der Académie Royale am 3. Mai 1742 folgendes Genehmigungsschreiben: „Meine Herren! Der Kupferstecher Herr Schmidt ersuchte den König, ihn mit der Ausnahme vom Gesetz zu begünstigen, ‚welches die Aufnahme der Protestanten in den Königlichen Academien untersagt', und zu erlauben, sich der Königlichen Academie der Künste vorstellen zu dürfen. Da nun Sr. Majestät für die besonderen Verdienste des Herrn Schmidt alle Achtung hegen, indem er sich bekanntlich in seiner Kunst ausgezeichnet hat, so bewilligten Sie seine Bitte." Zitiert nach L[udwig] D. Jacoby (Hrsg.): *Schmidt's Werke oder: beschreibendes Verzeichnis sämtlicher Kupferstiche und Radirungen, welche der berühmte Künstler George Friederich Schmidt, Königl. Preuss. Hofkupferstecher, Mitglied der Königl. Academien zu Berlin, Paris und der Kaiserlichen zu St. Petersburg von Anno 1729 bis zu seinem Tode 1775 verfertigt hat* (Berlin: In Jacoby's Kunsthandlung [...] und in Leipzig bei I. B. G. Fleischer 1815), 9–10. Vollwertiges Mitglied der Akademie wurde er aber erst im Jahre 1744, nachdem er sein Meisterstück, den Stich nach einem Bildnis des Malers Pierre Mignard, abgeliefert hatte. Vgl. Wessely: *Georg Friedrich Schmidt: Verzeichniss seiner Stiche und Radirungen*, XII.

phische Version seiner *Marriage A-la-Mode*-Serie auszuführen. Dazu dürfte er Schmidt in seinem Atelier besucht und diesen dort bei seiner aktuellen Arbeit am Porträt Friedrichs des Großen angetroffen haben. Womöglich erfuhr Hogarth von Schmidt, dass er auf seinem Stich das Antlitz des Monarchen – entsprechend den Porträtkonventionen der Zeit und orientiert an Pesnes Bruststück von 1738 – in stark geschönter Form wiedergab, ja dass der preußische König in Wirklichkeit viel hässlicher aussah und eine Adlernase besaß. Vielleicht bekam er vor Ort sogar Skizzen vom realen Aussehen Friedrichs zu Gesicht.

Ludwig D. Jacoby schreibt über Schmidt: „Unter seinen ausgezeichneten Talenten war auch das, richtig nach der Natur zu zeichnen, welches selbst bei den geschicktesten Kupferstechern nicht immer der Fall zu seyn pflegt."[70] Insofern darf man davon ausgehen, dass Schmidt – wie der für seine Charakterköpfe berühmte Hogarth auch – in der Lage war, die charakteristischen Gesichtszüge einer Person mit dem Zeichenstift einzufangen und somit das reale Aussehen Friedrichs korrekt darzustellen, auch wenn sich keine solchen Zeichnungen erhalten haben. Fraglich ist natürlich, ob der deutsche Künstler im Jahre 1743 den Preußenkönig wegen seines aktuellen Porträts persönlich kontaktiert hat und einige Skizzen von ihm anfertigte. Immerhin wird der Name „Schmidt" in Friedrichs „Schatullrechnungen" für den Mai 1743 genannt. Denkbar wäre auch, dass Schmidt den Monarchen zwar aufgesucht hat, der König aber wie üblich Porträtsitzungen ablehnte, was den Künstler jedoch nicht davon abgehalten haben muss, einige frische Skizzen anzufertigen, zumal er bekannt dafür war, sich ständig im Zeichnen zu üben.[71] Zudem kannte Schmidt den gleichaltrigen Kronprinzen noch aus seinen Berliner Tagen, so dass er – selbst aus der Erinnerung heraus – Hogarth mittels einiger Skizzen gezeigt haben könnte, wie Friedrichs Nase wirklich aussah.[72] Schmidt dürfte

---

70 Siehe Jacoby: *Schmidt's Werke oder: beschreibendes Verzeichnis sämtlicher Kupferstiche und Radirungen*, 11–12.

71 So ist z. B. überliefert, dass er und sein Künstlerkollege Johann Georg Wille „sich gegenseitig in allen möglichen Stellungen abzeichneten. Die schönsten Tage aber waren die, an denen sie bereits vor Tagesanbruch mit ihren Skizzenbüchern unter dem Arm aus den Toren wanderten, um den ganzen Tag sich in Feld und Wald herumzutreiben, hier ein malerisches Gärtnerhaus, dort eine anmutige Landschaft mit dem Stifte festhaltend und selbst die Ruhestunden der Förderung ihrer Kunst widmend." Siehe Seidel: *Friedrich der Grosse und die bildende Kunst*, 217.

72 Interessant ist unter diesem Gesichtspunkt auch eine Anekdote aus Schmidts späteren Petersburger Jahren: Der für kurze Zeit am Zarenhof tätige französische Maler Louis Tocqué hatte die russische Kaiserin Elisabeth mit einer „Stumpfnase", so wie er sie sah, porträtiert, was der Dargestellten missfiel, „die neben der Kaiserin doch auch ein Weib, und zudem ein sehr verliebtes Weib war. Sie wünschte, dass Schmidt wenigstens im Stich die Nase etwas verlängere, was dieser auch that, worüber Tocqué in Paris, als er Schmidt's Stich sah, sehr ungehalten war." Siehe Wessely: *Georg Friedrich Schmidt: Verzeichniss seiner Stiche und Radirungen*, XVII. Offenbar war der deutsche Künstler durchaus darin geübt, die von ihm Porträtierten in seinen Stichen mit attraktiveren Nasen zu versehen.

Hogarth auch über die homosexuellen Neigungen des Preußenkönigs unterrichtet haben, über die er aus erster Hand vielleicht mehr wusste, als bislang bekannt ist. Allein die Tatsache, dass Schmidt am gleichen Tag wie Friedrich geboren wurde[73] und den Kronprinzen schon in jungen Jahren kennen gelernt hatte, könnte darauf hindeuten, dass zwischen beiden Männern ein relativ intimes Verhältnis bestand. Von 1730 bis 1736 absolvierte Schmidt seinen preußischen Militärdienst, der jedoch durch die Fürsprache von Generalfeldmarschall von Grumbkow (etwa auf Veranlassung Friedrichs?) von vierzehn auf nur sechs Jahre verkürzt worden ist, damit er sich wieder verstärkt seinen künstlerischen Studien zuwenden konnte. Mit Georg Wenzeslaus von Knobelsdorff, der ursprünglich ebenfalls Soldat gewesen ist und mit dem Schmidt an der Berliner Kunstakademie studiert hatte, verband ihn eine lebenslange Freundschaft. Und von Knobelsdorff gehörte als königlicher Baumeister zum engsten Kreis der Männer um Friedrich. Nach seinem Weggang nach Paris wurde Schmidt vom Preußenkönig eine Weile finanziell unterstützt.[74] In der französischen Metropole wohnte er einige Jahre mit seinem Künstlerkollegen und Freund Johann Georg Wille in einer Männer-WG, in der es feucht-fröhlich zuging.[75] Vermutlich war diese Freundschaft intim. Äußerungen in Briefen deuten jedenfalls an, dass Wille "näher bey [Schmidt] gewesen" ist als man denkt,[76] ja dass Schmidt seine Ehe mit

---

73 Siehe Dehnert: "Georg Friedrich Schmidt, der Hofkupferstecher des Königs", 321.

74 Allerdings kam der Künstler mit dem kleinen Jahrgeld, das ihm Friedrich bewilligt hatte, nicht sehr weit, so dass er aus finanziellen Gründen in die Dienste Hyacinth Rigauds eintrat und dort so hervorragende Porträtstiche schuf, dass er einer der besten Kupferstecher von Paris wurde. Siehe Wessely: *Georg Friedrich Schmidt: Verzeichniss seiner Stiche und Radirungen*, IX–X. Vielleicht ist es kein Zufall, dass in der ersten Szene von Hogarth's *Marriage A-la-Mode* das Porträt eines Feldmarschalls im Stil von Rigaud an der Wand hängt, auf dem ein Kanonenrohr ironisch einen Penis imitiert. Siehe David Wykes: "Hogarth and Rigaud: One Portrait", *Notes and Queries* 36, Nr. 4 (Dezember 1989), 470–475.

75 Darüber berichtet Wille ausführlich in seinen Lebenserinnerungen, „in denen er mit besonderer Liebe bei der Schilderung seiner ersten Pariser Jahre und seines Freundes G. F. Schmidt verweilt". Siehe Seidel: *Friedrich der Grosse und die bildende Kunst*, 217. Vgl. Georges Duplessis (Hrsg.): *Mémoires et journal de J.-G. Wille, graveur du roi: publiés d'après les manuscrits autographes de la Bibliothèque Impériale*, 2 Bände (Paris: Jules Renouard 1857), wo oft von „mon ami Schmidt" die Rede ist.

76 In einem Brief vom 16. November 1746 gratuliert Wille zwar seinem Freund Schmidt zu seiner Hochzeit und wünscht ihm viel Glück mit seinem liebenswürdigen Frauenzimmer, „welches Von schöner gestalt, angenehmem Umgange und Vernünfftiger Aufferziehung ist", aber er ist auch deutlich verwirrt wegen der Neuigkeit: „[...] ich komme algemach zu mir selbst. Zwar es zancken sich verschiedene Dinge in mir. Ist es Freude und Vergnügen? Ist es Erstaunen und Verwunderung? [...] was hätten sie wohl dazu gesagt, wenn ich Von ohngefehr auff ihre hochzeit gekommen wäre, denn ich bin näher bey ihnen gewesen als sich wohl einbilden können." Offensichtlich deutet Wille hier an, dass seine Beziehung zu Schmidt nicht nur rein freundschaftlicher Natur, sondern sehr viel intimer gewesen ist. Weiter lässt Wille im gleichen Brief durchblicken, dass seine Brüder (ebenso wie Schmidt) vor allem wegen der hohen Mitgift geheiratet hätten. Über den einen von ihnen schreibt er: „Dreyßig Taußend Livers hat ihm seine Frau zugebracht. und seiner Frau Schwester ist Ein kränklicht Verhutzeltes mädchen wenn das stirbt, so hat er doppelt [...]" Siehe Elisabeth Decultot (Hrsg.): *Briefwechsel von Johann Georg Wille* (Tübingen: Max Niemeyer Verlag 1999), 67–68. Solche Bemerkungen in einem Gratulationsbrief zur Hochzeit klingen jedenfalls nicht danach, dass Wille der Ansicht war, sein Freund Schmidt hätte aus Liebe geheiratet.

Dorothee Luise Videbant 1746 vorrangig unter dem Gesichtspunkt der hohen Mitgift einging[77] und auch keine Skrupel hatte, seine Familie für längere Zeit zu verlassen, als er 1757 für einige Jahre nach St. Petersburg ging.[78]

Insofern wäre es durchaus möglich, dass Schmidt sogar mit Friedrich II., der ihn ja unter von Knobelsdorffs Mitwirkung nach Berlin zurückholte, ein sexuelles Verhältnis gehabt hat, auch wenn es dafür keine konkreten Belege gibt. Oder etwa doch? In einem Brief an Goethe schrieb Carl Friedrich Zelter über seinen Großonkel Schmidt, dass dieser „moralisch der Sinnesart seines Königs war, die eben nicht im Ansehn stand".[79] Meint Zelter hier mit umschreibenden Worten, dass beide Männer die gleichen sexuellen Neigungen teilten? Womöglich waren diese in der Familie Zelter bestens bekannt.[80] Dann wäre nicht auszuschließen, dass schon der junge Schmidt einer der „Favoriten" des preußischen Kronprinzen gewesen ist. Jedenfalls spricht einiges dafür, dass Hogarth seine internen Informationen über Friedrichs sexuelle Orientierung Schmidt zu verdanken hat, als er ihn in Paris wegen der geplanten Kupferstich-Version seiner sechsteiligen Bilderserie aufsuchte.[81]

77 In seinem Brief vom 1. November 1746 an Wille erwähnt Schmidt, dass er eine vermögende und liebreizende Frau geheiratet hat, und es ist offensichtlich, dass er seine Eheschließung vor allem „unter dem Gesichtspunkt der Mitgift und der dadurch gesicherten sozialen Stellung" betrachtete. Siehe Decultot: *Briefwechsel von Johann Georg Wille*, 23, 65–66, 689. Ob diese Vernunftehe glücklich war, wie einige spätere Biographen behauptet haben, ist nicht zweifelsfrei zu belegen, zumal auch von einem ungeratenen Sohn die Rede ist, der 19jährig verstarb. Dass Schmidt nach dem Tod seiner Frau ledig blieb, spricht eher dafür, dass er es vorrangig auf die Mitgift abgesehen hatte und nicht aus Sehnsucht nach dem weiblichen Geschlecht geheiratet hat.

78 Siehe Dehnert: "Georg Friedrich Schmidt, der Hofkupferstecher des Königs", 336.

79 Brief an Goethe vom 15. September 1831. Siehe Max Hecker (Hrsg.): *Der Briefwechsel zwischen Goethe und Zelter*, Dritter Band: 1828–1832 (Leipzig: Insel-Verlag 1918), 481. Dass der Hundenarr Friedrich seinem Stecher Schmidt 1749 eines seiner geliebten Windspiele schenken wollte, spricht auch für ein recht intimes Verhältnis beider Männer. Siehe Seidel: *Friedrich der Grosse und die bildende Kunst*, 220.

80 Wie gut Zelter durch Berichte von Friedrich Gottlieb Berger (dessen Sohn Daniel ein Schüler und Mitarbeiter von Schmidt gewesen ist) über das Privatleben des deutschen Künstlers Bescheid wusste, geht auch aus den Anekdoten hervor, die er über Schmidt im gleichen Brief an Goethe zum Besten gibt, etwa über die derben Scherze, die der Berliner Künstler – ähnlich wie Hogarth! – mit einigen Zeitgenossen trieb. Zum Beispiel schoss Schmidt von seinem Fenster aus einem Schiffer mit seinem Luftgewehr eine Wachskugel ins nackte Hinterteil, als dieser von Bord seines Kahns aus seine Notdurft verrichtete. Siehe Hecker (Hrsg.): *Der Briefwechsel zwischen Goethe und Zelter*, Dritter Band, 481–483. Zu Hogarths ähnlich derbem Humor: Bernd W. Krysmanski: *Hogarth's Hidden Parts: Satiric Allusion, Erotic Wit, Blasphemous Bawdiness and Dark Humour in Eighteenth-Century English Art* (Hildesheim, Zürich, New York: Georg Olms Verlag 2010).

81 Zwar belegt kein einziges schriftliches Dokument ein konkretes Treffen von Hogarth mit Schmidt oder den anderen Pariser Künstlern, doch ist davon auszugehen, dass der Engländer, der sich nachweislich im Mai und Juni 1743 nach geeigneten Kupferstechern in Paris umgesehen hat, auch auf den deutschen Künstler gestoßen sein muss, der laut Goethe „einer der größten" gewesen ist, „dessen sich die Kupferstecherkunst zu rühmen hat; er wußte die genaueste Reinlichkeit und zugleich Festigkeit des Grabstichels mit einer Bewegung, einer Behandlung zu verbinden, welche sowohl kühn, als abwechselnd [...] war, immer aber vom höchsten Geschmack und Wissen. Von dem regelmäßigen Schnitt, worin er den ernstesten Chalkographen nacheiferte, ging er, nach Belieben, zur freien Behandlung über, indem er sich jenes spielenden Punctirens der geistreichsten Radirkünstler bediente und das Urtheil ungewiß ließ, ob

Dass Hogarth in Schmidts Atelier aufgetaucht sein muss, belegt eine Anzeige vom 8. November 1744 im *Daily Advertiser*, die erwähnt, dass sich im Juni 1743 Bernard Baron, Simon François Ravenet, Louis Gérard Scotin, Jacques Philippe Le Bas, ein Stecher namens Dupré (wohl eine Verwechslung mit Nicolas Gabriel Dupuis) und „Suberan" (= Pierre Soubeyran, ein Schüler von Schmidt!) bereit erklärt hatten, für Hogarth zu arbeiten und je eine Platte seiner sechsteiligen Serie zu übernehmen.[82] Doch wegen des Krieges mit Frankreich konnten die drei letztgenannten Stecher ihre Zusage nicht einhalten, weil sie außerstande waren, zur Ausführung von Paris nach London zu kommen, weshalb sich die Fertigstellung der Stiche verzögerte.[83] Wenn Hogarth in seiner Anzeige Schmidts Schüler Soubeyran namentlich nennt, muss er 1743 das Pariser Atelier des deutschen Meisters besucht haben und dort auch mit Schmidt selbst über dessen aktuelles Friedrich-Porträt und die geplante Stichversion der *Marriage A-la-Mode*-Serie gesprochen haben. Nicht nur das: Auch wegen ihres ähnlich zotigen Humors müssten sich Schmidt und Hogarth in Paris prächtig verstanden haben. Da beide das feucht-fröhliche Tavernenleben schätzten, ist anzunehmen, dass der englische Künstler dem seelenverwandten Deutschen beim gemeinsamen Gläschen auch einige intime Details über das Leben des Preußenkönigs entlocken konnte. Dass Hogarth in der Lage gewesen sein muss, sich mit Schmidt auf Französisch zu verständigen, geht aus seiner handschriftlich überlieferten Übersetzung von Claude-Henri Watelet's *L'art de peindre* (1760) hervor.[84]

Der Künstler war wohl sauer auf den Preußenkönig

Doch eine definitive Zusage, mindestens eines der *Marriage A-la-Mode*-Bilder zu stechen, durfte Hogarth letztlich von Schmidt nicht erhalten haben, denn der deutsche Künstler verließ Paris und kehrte nach Berlin zu Fried-

er sich in einer oder der andern Art vorzüglicher bewiesen habe." Perfekt beherrschte er die einfühlende Zeichnung und das Helldunkel. Siehe Johann Wolfgang von Goethe: "Georg Friedrich Schmidt, geboren Berlin 1712, abgegangen daselbst 1775", in: *Goethe's Werke: Vollständige Ausgabe letzter Hand*, Drey und vierzigster Band (Stuttgart und Tübingen: in der J. G. Cotta'schen Buchhandlung 1833), 227–228. Insofern wäre ein Mann mit diesen Fähigkeiten genau der Richtige gewesen, die Stichversion von *Marriage A-la-Mode* auszuführen, was Hogarth, der ja selbst das Stecherhandwerk hervorragend beherrschte, sicher nicht entgangen sein dürfte.

82 Vgl. Paulson: *Hogarth, Volume 2: High Art and Low, 1732–1750*, 211; Simon: "Un rosbif à Paris: Hogarth's visit to Paris in 1743", 24, 29–30; ders.: *Hogarth, France and British Art*, 27, 35.

83 Ursprünglich hatte Hogarth geplant, seine Gemälde nach Paris zu transportieren und sie dort stechen zu lassen, doch der zwischenzeitlich ausgebrochene Krieg verhinderte dies. So wurden die Stichversionen der sechs Szenen letztlich nur von drei französischen Stechern, nämlich Baron, Ravenet und Scotin in London unter Hogarths Aufsicht ausgeführt.

84 Siehe John A. Dussinger: "William Hogarth's translation of Watelet on 'Grace' ", *Burlington Magazine* 126 (1984), 691–694.

rich dem Großen zurück. Am 6. Juli 1743 wurde das Ernennungspatent zum Hofkupferstecher ausgestellt, das ihm 600 Taler Gehalt zusicherte.[85] Vielleicht hatte er sogar anfänglich zugesagt, für Hogarth zu arbeiten, dies aber kurze Zeit später wegen des lukrativeren Angebots aus Berlin wieder ausgeschlagen.[86] Diese Abwerbung würde auch erklären, warum Hogarth den Preußenkönig mit einer gehörigen Portion Wut im Bauch als eine Art Gegenentwurf zum idealisierenden Friedrich-Porträt von Schmidt, nämlich als älter wirkenden, päderastischen Flötisten, in seine *Marriage A-la-Mode*-Serie aufgenommen hat. Es ist bekannt, dass der englische Künstler in vergleichbaren Situationen ähnlich unwirsch reagierte und dazu neigte, Zeitgenossen in seinen Werken mit dem Pinsel und dem Grabstichel zu verunglimpfen, wenn diese nicht in seinem Sinne handelten oder er sie aus anderen Gründen nicht leiden konnte.[87] Andererseits wimmelt es in Hogarths Bildern nur so von Darstellungen populärer Zeitgenossen oder von Personen aus seinem Umfeld, die er offenbar zu seiner persönlichen Belustigung in seine figurenreichen Bilder aufgenommen hat – als wollte er den Betrachter animieren, nach bekannten Gesichtern in seinen Werken zu suchen.[88]

---

85 Zum französischen Originalwortlaut des Dokuments: Schepkowski: *Johann Ernst Gotzkowsky*, 248n932.

86 Dies könnte auch der Grund dafür sein, dass Hogarth als Alternative Schmidts Schüler Soubeyran verpflichten wollte, wobei dieser dann nur die zweite Wahl gewesen wäre.

87 In einem zeitgenössischen Nachruf auf Hogarth lesen wir, dass der Künstler, nachdem ihn einst seine Zimmerwirtin wegen der lächerlichen Summe von 20 Schillingen verhaften ließ und er sich von einem Freund auslösen lassen musste, die betreffende Frau aus Rache so hässlich wie möglich dargestellt hat, „or, as painters express it, in *Caricatura*." Siehe "Memoirs of Mr. William Hogarth", *Annual Register* 7 (Dezember 1764), 62. Ein andermal hatte Hogarth einen Edelmann so realistisch mit all seinen natürlichen Deformationen gemalt, so dass der Porträtierte sich weigerte, das Bild zu bezahlen. Hogarth drohte daraufhin, das Bildnis mit einem Schwanz und einigen anderen kleineren Anhängseln zu versehen und es bei „Mr. Hare", dem „wild-beast man", öffentlich auszustellen, wenn das Geld nicht innerhalb von drei Tagen einträfe. Die Drohung hatte den gewünschten Erfolg: Der Lord zahlte den Betrag in voller Höhe. Vgl. John Nichols/George Steevens: *The Genuine Works of William Hogarth*, 2 Bände (London: Printed for Longman, Hurst, Rees, and Orme 1808–1810), Band I, 24–25. Das Gemälde *The Gate of Calais* (1748; Tate Britain, London) entstand kurz nach Hogarths zweiter Frankreich-Tour als Antwort auf seine schlechte Behandlung am anderen Kanalufer. Die französische Festungswache hatte den Künstler beim Skizzieren vor Ort als vermeintlichen Spion verhaftet und auf höchst unrühmliche Weise des Landes verwiesen. Als Antwort stellte er besonders dürre, ausgemergelte, zur Homosexualität neigende französische Soldaten vor dem Tor von Calais dar, wie sie einem riesigen Stück Rindfleisch nachgaffen, das für englische Lebensqualität und Freiheit steht. Näheres hierzu bei Bernd Krysmanski: "*O the Roast Beef of Old England:* Hogarth in BSEfreier Zeit vor dem Tor von Calais", *Lichtenberg-Jahrbuch 1997* (Saarbrücken: Saarbrücker Druckerei und Verlag 1998), 29–52; Dominic Janes, "Unnatural Appetites: Sodomitical Panic in Hogarth's *The Gate of Calais, or, O the Roast Beef of Old England* (1748)", *Oxford Art Journal* 35, Nr. 1 (2012), 19–31. In *The Bruiser* (1763) taucht Charles Churchill als betrunkener Bär im Bild auf, während Hogarths Hund auf ein gegen den Künstler gerichtetes Schmähgedicht pinkelt, das Churchill verfasst hatte. Siehe Paulson: *Hogarth's Graphic Works*, Nr. 213. Weitere Beispiele bei Krysmanski: *Hogarth's Hidden Parts*, 59–66.

88 So trägt in *The Gate of Calais* der an zentraler Stelle dargestellte Mönch die Züge des Kupferstechers John Pine, der daraufhin den Spitznamen „Friar Pine" nicht mehr loswurde. Siehe Nichols/ Steevens: *The Genuine Works of William Hogarth*, Band I, 147–148. Bei dem Prediger, der in *The Sleeping Congregation* (1736) eine einschläfernde Predigt hält, soll es sich um John Theophilus Desaguliers handeln, damals ein führendes Mitglied der englischen Freimaurerbewegung. Siehe Bernd Krysmanski: "Lust in Hogarth's *Sleeping Con-*

Dass Hogarth in der Lage war, die Gesichtszüge seiner Zeitgenossen älter darzustellen, als sie in Wirklichkeit waren, geht aus einigen Bemerkungen in seiner Schrift *The Analysis of Beauty* (1753) hervor. Der Künstler beschreibt dort im Kapitel „Of the Face", „auf welche Weise sich die Linien des Gesichts von der Kindheit an mit den Jahren ändern, und die unterschiedlichen Alter im einzelnen bezeichnen": „Im Alter zwischen zwanzig und dreißig treten [...] nur wenige Veränderungen auf." Danach aber „werden die Veränderungen immer sichtbarer. Wir bemerken, daß die klare Einfachheit von vielen gerundeten Teilen des Gesichts in voneinander geschiedene Formen mit abrupteren Windungen um die Muskeln herum übergeht", bis dann im Alter von über fünfzig die „Falten und Kerben im Gesicht" immer deutlicher hervortreten und zuletzt nur „ein reizvolles Stück von Ruinen" übrig bleibt.[89] Insofern mag Hogarth den Preußenkönig auf seinem Bild bewusst älter dargestellt und auch ein wenig karikaturhaft verzeichnet haben – fast wie mit einem modernen Bildbearbeitungsprogramm, das junge Gesichter alter wirken lasst, so wie sie zukünftig aussehen werden. Womöglich aber sah Friedrich in jüngeren Jahren schon ziemlich alt aus, so dass Hogarth die tatsächlichen Gesichtszüge des Preußenkönigs wesentlich besser getroffen haben könnte als Schmidt mit seinem jugendlich wirkenden, unrealistischen Bildnis.

Könnte es darüber hinaus sein, dass nicht nur Friedrich II., sondern auch sein frisch gebackener Hofstecher als Homosexueller in Hogarths Bild aufgenommen wurde? Ist etwa der effeminierte Mann mit dem Fächer am Handgelenk, der weiter hinten dem Kastraten zuwinkt, eine Karikatur auf Schmidt?

Vergleicht man Hogarths Darstellung eines homosexuellen Mannes mit Schmidts Jahre später in Rembrandtmanier radiertem *Selbstbildnis „mit der Spinne"* (1758),[90] finden sich immerhin folgende Übereinstimmungen: das

gregation – Or, How to Waste Time in Post-Puritan England", *Art History* 21, Nr. 3 (September 1998), 406n27. In etlichen Bildern tauchen stadtbekannte Personen aus dem Londoner Prostituiertenmilieu auf, so der Mädchenschänder Colonel Charteris und die Kupplerin "Mother Needham" in *A Harlot's Progress*, Plate 1 (1732). Der Politiker, der in *Chairing the Members* (1758) als Wahlsieger durch die Gegend geschaukelt wird, ist George Bubb Dodington. Unter den Charakterköpfen in *The Bench* (1758) finden sich so hochgestellte Persönlichkeiten wie Chief Justice Sir John Willes oder Sir Edward Clive. In der zweiten Illustration zur *Analysis of Beauty* (1753) wird der künftige König Georg III. als elegant tanzender Prince of Wales neben anderen, ungelenk-steif agierenden Tänzern dargestellt. In *The First Stage of Cruelty* (1751) soll derselbe Prinz als Knabe repräsentiert sein, wie er – in diesem Fall als moralisches Vorbild – brutale Jugendliche von der Misshandlung von Tieren abzuhalten versucht. Siehe Paulson: *Hogarth's Graphic Works*, 78, 168, 171, 160, 149.

89 William Hogarth: *Analyse der Schönheit. Aus dem Englischen von Jörg Heininger. Mit einem Nachwort von Peter Bexte* (Dresden: Verlag der Kunst 1995), 183–184. Vgl. zum Originalwortlaut: William Hogarth: *The Analysis of Beauty, with the Rejected Passages from the Manuscript Drafts and Autobiographical Notes*, hrsg. von Joseph Burke (Oxford: Clarendon Press 1955), 142, 144–45; ders.: *The Analysis of Beauty*, hrsg. von Ronald Paulson (New Haven und London: Yale University Press 1997), 99, 101.

90 Siehe Kirsten Ahrens: *Georg Friedrich Schmidt: Selbstbildnis mit der Spinne, Aus dem Bestand des Porträtarchivs Diepenbroick im Westfälischen Landesmuseum für Kunst und Kulturgeschichte [Das Kunstwerk* rundliche Gesicht, der relativ schmale Mund mit seinen dennoch vollen Lippen, eine ähnliche Nasenform und deutlich sichtbare Augenringe,[91] wobei die Details von Hogarth satirisch überzeichnet wurden, um das Weibische im Manne zu unterstreichen. Nicht zufällig dürfte sich bei beiden Personen auch die Art des um den Hals eng geschlossenen weißen Rüschenhemdes ähneln. Man achte ferner auf die ausdrucksstark dargestellten Hände, die in Schmidts Selbstporträt betonen, wie wichtig sie für den Künstler sind. Auch Hogarth betont die Hände, doch steht bei ihm ironisch der feminine Winkgestus im Vordergrund, der eine gleichgeschlechtliche Kontaktaufnahme einleiten soll. Hatte etwa Schmidt keinen Hehl aus seinen sexuellen Neigungen gemacht, so dass er dem Betrachter hier von Hogarth so unverblümt als schwul präsentiert werden konnte?

Simon François Ravenet nach William Hogarth: *Marriage A-la-Mode*, Plate 4 (1745). Ausschnitt.

Georg Friedrich Schmidt: *Selbstbildnis „mit der Spinne"* (1758)

Falls mit dem winkenden Mann, der als Zugabe ein Schönheitspflästerchen an der Unterlippe trägt und dessen Nase obendrein leicht syphilitisch deformiert erscheint,[92] tatsächlich Schmidt gemeint sein sollte, dann wäre dieser von Ho-

---

des Monats/Westfälisches Landesmuseum für Kunst und Kulturgeschichte Münster, Landschaftsverband Westfalen-Lippe, Oktober 1990]; Gisold Lammel: *Tagträume: Bilder im Lichte der Aufklärung* (Dresden: Verlag der Kunst 1993), 40.

91 Diese Augenringe scheinen ein charakteristisches Merkmal von Schmidt gewesen zu sein. Wir finden sie auch in seinem Selbstporträt von 1752.

92 Solche Nebenmotive, die auf die Symptome der Geschlechtskrankheit selbst verweisen oder – wie im Falle der dunklen Schönheitspflästerchen – unerwünschte Hautausschläge und die Spuren der falschen ärztlichen Behandlung verdecken sollen, tauchen in Hogarths Oeuvre ständig auf. Siehe Egerton: "Zu garth nicht nur eindeutig als promisker Homosexueller ausgewiesen worden, sondern auch die ideale Begleitfigur für den Flöte spielenden Alten Fritz![93]

Wie dem auch sei: Die Perücke, die Hogarths Flötist trägt, ähnelt der Perücke, die der junge Preußenkönig auf Schmidts Porträt trägt. Dass bei Hogarth die Perücke des Flötisten grauer wirkt als die anderen Perücken im Bild, könnte daran liegen, dass dem Künstler bekannt war, dass der modisch äußerst nachlässige Friedrich eine ungepflegte, nicht regelmäßig gepuderte Zopfperücke trug.[94] Auch die schlichte Kleidung des Flötenspielers könnte auf die bekannte Tatsache anspielen, dass der Monarch meist recht einfach gewandet war.[95] Und die übertrieben große Hakennase wurde dem Querflöte spielenden Friedrich vor allem deswegen verpasst, um eine direkte Verbindung zum Adler-Schnabel auf dem *Ganymed*-Bild herzustellen. Vergessen wir in diesem Zusammenhang auch nicht, dass ein gekrönter schwarzer Adler jahrhundertelang das imposante Wappentier des Königreichs Preußen gewesen ist – ein Adler, wie er auch in Schmidts Friedrich-Porträt von 1743 auftaucht.

Crébillons "Le Sopha" – ein Hinweis auf den Alten Fritz

Als weiterer dezenter Hinweis auf die Anwesenheit des preußischen Monarchen in Hogarths Bild liegt auf dem Sofa, von dem aus der Ehebruch der Gräfin eingeleitet wird, ein Buch mit der Aufschrift [Le] *Sopha*.

William Hogarths Zyklus *Marriage A-la-Mode*", 29, 33–34; N. F. Lowe: "Hogarth, Beauty Spots, and sexually transmitted Diseases", *British Journal for Eighteenth Century Studies* 15, Nr. 1 (Spring 1992), 71–79; ders.: "The Meaning of Venereal Disease in Hogarth's Graphic Art", in: Linda E. Merians (Hrsg.): *The Secret Malady. Venereal Disease in Eighteenth Century Britain and France* (Lexington: University Press of Kentucky 1996), 168–182; Fiona Haslam: *From Hogarth to Rowlandson. Medicine in Art in Eighteenth-Century Britain* (Liverpool: Liverpool University Press 1996); Peter Wagner: "Spotting the Symptoms: Hogarthian Bodies as Sites of Semantic Ambiguity", in: Bernadette Fort/Angela Rosenthal (Hrsg.): *The Other Hogarth: Aesthetics of Difference* (Princeton: Princeton University Press 2001), 102–119.

93 Dennoch muss die Identifizierung des Manns mit dem Fächer in Hogarths Bild spekulativ bleiben. Sie basiert nur auf einem vagen Vergleich mit Schmidts *Selbstbildnis „mit der Spinne"*. Durch zeitgenössische Dokumente ist sie nicht belegt. Allerdings kann man sich des Eindrucks kaum erwehren, dass Schmidt, der stets zu Scherzen aufgelegt war, sich in Hogarths Darstellung wiedererkannt haben könnte und nun im Selbstporträt dem Betrachter mit seinem Zeigegestus sagen will: „Seht genau hin! Hielt diese Hand bei Hogarth nicht eine Tasse und die andere, winkende Hand einen Fächer?" Die Spinne im Bildnis ist übrigens auch ein Detail, das von Hogarth entlehnt sein dürfte. Vgl. Paulson: *Hogarth's Graphic Works*, Nr. 136 u. 163.

94 Laut Groth soll der Alte Fritz „eine Perücke mit Zopf" getragen haben, „der die mangelnde Pflege nur zu deutlich anzusehen war." Siehe Groth: "Wie Friedrich II. wirklich aussah".

95 Zeitgenossen berichten etwa, dass Friedrich im Gegensatz zu anderen Monarchen wenig Zeit mit der Toilette verbrachte, ohne aufwendiges Ankleiden auskam und alte, verschmutzte Uniformen trug. Siehe Ute Christina Koch: " ,Un jour comme l'autre': Ein Tag im Leben Friedrichs in Berichten des 18. und frühen 19. Jahrhunderts". In: *Friederisiko: Friedrich der Große*, Ausst.-Kat., Stiftung Preußische Schlösser und Gärten Berlin-Brandenburg im Neuen Palais und Park Sanssouci, 28. April–28. Oktober 2012, 2 Bände (München: Hirmer 2012), Band I: *Die Ausstellung*, 315.

Es stammt aus der Feder von Claude Prosper Jolyot de Crébillon, erschien 1742 und wurde angeblich von Friedrich dem Großen in Auftrag gegeben.[96] In dieser Parodie auf die *Märchen aus Tausend und einer Nacht* wird geschildert, was die Seele des Lüstlings Amanzéi erlebt, die vom Gott Brahma in ein

Simon François Ravenet nach William Hogarth: *Marriage A-la-Mode*, Plate 4 (1745). Ausschnitt.

Sofa verbannt wurde und erst dann wieder erlöst wird, wenn ein wahrhaft unschuldiges Paar auf dem Sofa seine erste ehrliche Liebe erlebt. Doch es dauert recht lange, bis dies geschieht, und das Sofa muss etliche unkeusch-laszive Szenen miterleben. Dass dieses Buch in Hogarths Darstellung als Ne-

---

96 Vgl. Viktor Link: "The Reception of Crébillon's *Le Sopha* in England: An Unnoticed Edition and Some Imitations", *Studies on Voltaire and the Eighteenth Century* 132 (1975), 199–203; Martina Ochs: "Sexualität in *Le Sopha* von Crébillon Fils", Studienarbeit, Universität des Saarlandes (München: GRIN, 1995); Carole Dornier: "Orient romanesque et satire de la religion: Claude Crébillon: *Tanzaï et Néadarné* et *Le Sopha*", *Eighteenth-Century Fiction* 11, Nr. 4 (1999), 445–459.

benmotiv auftaucht, kann kein Zufall sein. Und noch ein schlagendes Argument spricht dafür, dass Hogarth in seiner Szene den Alten Fritz dargestellt hat: Niemand anders würde mit seiner Flöte besser zwischen das päderastische Bild mit dem Adler und den vor ihm sitzenden Kastraten passen!

Auch in anderen Werken von Hogarth taucht Friedrich II. auf

Dass sich der Künstler auch an anderer Stelle mit dem Preußenkönig beschäftigt hat, geht aus der ironischen Widmung zur graphischen Version seines *March to Finchley* (1750/51) hervor. Dort heißt es: „To His Majesty the King of Prus[s]ia, an Encourager of Arts and Sciences! This Plate is most Humbly Dedicated".[97] Mit dem rund ein Jahr früher entstandenen Gemälde gleichen Titels (London, Foundling Museum) hatte Hogarth an die schottische Gefahr der Jahre 1745/46 erinnert, gegen die die englischen Grenadiere – teils noch betrunken, teils mit ihren Liebchen, mit Urinieren oder anderweitig beschäftigt – zusammengetrommelt werden und ausmarschieren, um unter der Führung des Duke of Cumberland letztlich in der Schlacht von Culloden die schottischen Rebellen zu besiegen, die vom katholischen Kronprätendenten angeführt wurden. Zentral im Getümmel muss sich bei Hogarth ein Soldat wie ein „Herkules am Scheidewege" zwischen einer patriotischen Schwangeren und einer älteren Katholikin entscheiden. Die relative Unordnung im Vordergrund lässt sich mit der in Rembrandts *Nachtwache* (1642; Rijksmuseum, Amsterdam) vergleichen und stimmte den militaristisch gesinnten König Georg II., dem die Stichversion des Bildes zugeeignet werden sollte, nicht gerade freundlich, zumal er ein Kunstbanause war, der mit Malerei und Dichtung nur wenig anfangen konnte. Angeblich hat Georg, der eine strenge hannoveranische Militärdisziplin gewöhnt war, vor allem das ungeordnete Treiben auf dem Bild moniert, das seine Gardesoldaten verhöhnt, und deswegen eine Widmung mit seinem Namen abgelehnt, weshalb Hogarth den von Luke Sullivan ausgeführten Nachstich ironisch Friedrich dem Großen, dem wahren Förderer der Künste, widmete.[98]

---

97 Zur Stichversion von Luke Sullivan nach Hogarths Gemälde (Foundling Museum, London) siehe Paulson: *Hogarth's Graphic Works*, 141–145, Nr. 184.

98 Siehe John Ireland: *Hogarth Illustrated*, 2 Bände, 2. Aufl. (London: J. and J. Boydell 1793), Band II, 132–133; Paulson: *Hogarth's Graphic Works*, 142. Die neuere Forschung bezweifelt jedoch diese Anekdote. Vgl. Elizabeth Einberg: "Milton, St. John and the importance of 'Bottom': Another look at Hogarth's *March of the Guards to Finchley*", *The British Art Journal* 5, Nr. 3 (Winter 2004), 27–34; Robert Mode: "Still 'Marching to Finchley': Hogarth, Coram, and the Two Fredericks", in Bernd W. Krysmanski (Hrsg.): *250 Years On: New Light on William Hogarth* (in Vorbereitung). Nach Elizabeth Einbergs Ansicht könnte Hogarth mit seinem Gemälde, das ja ganz gezielt auf eine Militäraktion bezugnimmt, die der Duke of Cumberland, Georgs Sohn, erfolgreich durchführte, auf königliche Patronage gehofft haben, was aber gründlich misslang. Interessant ist auch, dass Paul Sandbys Anti-Hogarth-Karikatur *The Painter's March from Finchly* (1754) ironisch dem „König der Zigeuner als Förderer der Künste" gewidmet ist. Siehe Ronald Paulson:

Luke Sullivan nach William Hogarth: *The March to Finchley* (1750/51)

Mehr als zehn Jahre später stellt Hogarth im Vordergrund von *The Times*, Plate 1 (1762)[99] – einem propagandistischen Stich, der die Befürworter des Siebenjährigen Krieges als Weltbrand-Anheizer attackiert – Friedrich den Großen als Fiedler dar, auch hier charakteristischerweise mit relativ großer Nase. Er sitzt, einen Dreispitz tragend, wie ein verarmter Straßenmusiker zwischen verzweifelten Frauen und Kindern, die mit ihrer letzten Habe die vom Krieg verwüsteten Häuser verlassen mussten.

Vermutlich handelt es sich bei diesem Motiv um eine Anspielung darauf, dass der Earl of Bute,[100] ein enger Vertrauter von König Georg III., dem mit

---

Hogarth, *Volume 3: Art and Politics, 1750–1764* (Cambridge: Lutterworth Press 1993), 135–136 und Abb. 32; Douglas Fordham: *British Art and the Seven Years' War: Allegiance and Autonomy* (Philadelphia: University of Pennsylvania Press, 2010), 59–60.

99 Siehe Nichols: *Biographical Anecdotes of William Hogarth*, 71–72, 300–304, 451–457; Paulson: *Hogarth's Graphic Works*, Nr. 211; ders.: *Hogarth, Volume 3: Art and Politics, 1750–1764*, 370–387.

100 John Stuart, Third Earl of Bute (1713–1792), hatte Georg III. erzogen, war nach dessen Thronbesteigung 1760 zunächst Staatssekretär und für kurze Zeit, nämlich vom 26. Mai 1762 bis zum 18. April 1763, englischer Premierminister.

William Hogarth: *The Times*, Plate 1 (1762)

England verbündeten Preußen in der Endphase des Siebenjährigen Krieges die Hilfsgelder verweigerte,[101] um Friedrich II., der auf dem Kontinent gegen Frankreich, Österreich und Russland kämpfte, zum Frieden zu zwingen. Trost findet der Preußenkönig in dieser misslichen Situation allein in der Musik.

Interessant ist, dass die Widmung unter dem *March to Finchley* den Alten Fritz ironisch als Förderer der Künste und Wissenschaften herausstellt und der Geiger in *The Times*, Plate 1, die Liebe des Monarchen zur Musik auch unter brenzligen Umständen betont. Insofern ist es mehr als wahrscheinlich, dass Hogarth den Alten Fritz bereits in der vierten Szene seiner *Marriage-A-la-Mode*-Folge satirisch als Flötisten den anderen Homosexuellen zugesellt hat, die dort den gehörnten, pädophilen Grafen flankieren, um dadurch spöttisch auf abweichende sexuelle Verhaltensweisen aufmerksam

---

101 Friedrich II. hatte 1758–1762 von England Subsidien angenommen. Siehe Bringmann: *Preußen unter Friedrich Wilhelm II.*, 503. Zum Bündnisbruch 1762: Katja Frehland-Wildeboer: *Treue Freunde? Das Bündnis in Europa, 1714–1914* (München: Oldenbourg Wissenschaftsverlag 2010), 113; Kurt Kluxen: *Geschichte Englands: Von den Anfängen bis zur Gegenwart* (Stuttgart: Kröner 1968), 450–451.

zu machen, wie sie damals ungeniert und ungehemmt in hohen Kreisen ausgelebt wurden. Schließlich war Friedrich der prominenteste Schwule seiner Zeit und daher geradezu prädestiniert, auf einem Bild aufzutauchen, das die Schwächen der adligen Gesellschaft anprangert.

William Hogarth: *The Times*, Plate 1 (1762). Ausschnitt.

Das Besondere an Hogarths Darstellung

Wahrscheinlich handelt es sich bei Hogarths Darstellung um die realistischste Wiedergabe des Preußenkönigs, die je von einem Künstler gemalt oder gestochen wurde. Die meisten anderen Porträts geben ja, wie wir eingangs hörten, Friedrichs Antlitz nicht naturalistisch, sondern viel zu idealisiert wieder. Dies entsprach der Konvention der Zeit, die zwischen dem „corpus politicum" und dem „corpus naturale" unterschied, d. h., zwischen dem Herrscher als Repräsentanten eines überindividuellen, gleichsam gottgegebenen Amtes, der deswegen im Bilde auch unrealistisch-überhöht darzustellen war, und der sterblichen, realen Erscheinung des Monarchen, die mit dem „politischen Körper" nichts zu tun hatte.[102] Frauke Mankartz glaubt daher, dass Friedrich sich den Porträts seines „corpus naturale" überwiegend entziehen konnte, ansonsten aber seine „königlichen Repräsentationspflichten" insofern erfüllt habe, als er seinen „ ‚politischen Körper' [...] für

---

102 Siehe Rainer Schoch: *Das Herrscherbild in der Malerei des 19. Jahrhunderts* (München: Prestel Verlag 1975), 13, 22, 108; Ernst Hartwig Kantorowicz: *Die zwei Körper des Königs: Eine Studie zur politischen Theologie des Mittelalters. Aus dem Amerikanischen übersetzt von Walter Theimer (Stuttgart: Klett-Cotta 1992).*

Amtsporträts zur Verfügung stellte",[103] sich dabei aber bewusst war, dass diese von seinem „natürlichen Körper" stark abwichen.[104] So ließ er sich denn auch nicht lumpen, kostbar verzierte Dosen mit seinem Bildnis und später auch Porzellan- oder Bronzestatuetten, die ihn zu Pferde zeigten, an Diplomaten und andere hochrangige Persönlichkeiten zu verschenken.[105] Offenbar schien es kaum jemanden zu stören, dass der Alte Fritz auf solchen Repräsentationsbildern, die fast schon wie heutige Firmengeschenke und Fanartikel zirkulierten, ganz anders als in natura aussah.

Für Hogarth jedoch, der sich mit den realen Physiognomien seiner Mitmenschen beschäftigte, ja sehr genau zwischen Charakterköpfen und Karikaturen differenzierte,[106] ist die alte Unterscheidung zwischen dem überindividuellen Amt und der wirklichen Person eines Monarchen, die für die Produktion idealisierter Bildnisse verantwortlich war, nicht mehr relevant gewesen. Ihm kam es allein auf das reale Antlitz der Zeitgenossen an, mochten diese so hochgestellt sein, wie sie wollten. Insofern machte er auch bei Friedrich dem Großen keine Ausnahme und stellte ihn so hässlich dar, wie er in Wirklichkeit aussah – ja, weil er aus persönlichen Gründen sauer auf ihn war, wohl noch eine Spur hässlicher.

Es wäre sogar möglich, dass für die Aufnahme des Preußenkönigs in Hogarths Bild auch aktuelle politische Gründe eine Rolle gespielt haben. Die Situation auf dem Kontinent war zur Entstehungszeit der *Marriage-A-la-Mode*-Gemälde (1743/44), also zwischen dem Ersten und Zweiten Schlesischen Krieg, ziemlich unübersichtlich. Politische Allianzen wechselten ständig.[107] Friedrich der Große hatte sich dabei vor allem mit Österreich auseinanderzusetzen. Am 23. September 1743 verbündete sich Maria Theresia mit Großbritannien, was den Preußenkönig veranlasste, sich nach neuen Bundesgenossen umzusehen. Einen solchen Bündnispartner fand er ausgerechnet in Frankreich, gegen das kurz zuvor noch Georg II. von England persönlich

---

103 Vgl. Frauke Mankartz: "Die Marke Friedrich: Der preußische König im zeitgenössischen Bild", in: *Friederisiko: Friedrich der Große*, Ausst.-Kat., Stiftung Preußische Schlösser und Gärten Berlin-Brandenburg im Neuen Palais und Park Sanssouci, 28. April–28. Oktober 2012, 2 Bände (München: Hirmer 2012), Band I: *Die Ausstellung*, 209.

104 Zu einem von Anna Dorothea Therbusch gemalten Porträt, das er 1775 Voltaire schickte, bemerkte Friedrich: "Um ihren Pinsel nicht zu entehren, hat sie mein verzerrtes Gesicht wieder mit der Grazie der Jugend aufgeschmückt." Siehe ebda., 209, Abb. 8.

105 Ebda., 212, 218.

106 Vgl. sein Blatt *Characters and Caricaturas* (1743), das als Subskriptionsquittung für die Stichversion der *Marriage-A-la-Mode*-Serie diente. Siehe Paulson: *Hogarth's Graphic Works*, Nr. 156; ders.: *Hogarth, Volume 2: High Art and Low, 1732–1750*, 206–208; Cowley: *Marriage A-la-Mode*, 17-20.

107 Eine Übersicht über die für uns relevanten Kriegsereignisse findet sich etwa bei Karl Adolf Menzel: *Neuere Geschichte der Deutschen von der Reformation bis zur Bundes-Acte*, Zehnter Band: *Die Zeit Karls VI. und die Anfänge Friedrichs II.* (Breslau: Druck und Verlag von Graß, Barth und Comp. 1843), 435 ff.

gekämpft hatte. Mit gut Glück konnte König Georg am 27. Juni 1743 in der Schlacht bei Dettingen mit seinen britisch-hannoveranischen Truppen das französische Heer bezwingen, was auf der britischen Insel gebührend gefeiert wurde.[108] Doch auf den Allianzvertrag zwischen Maria Theresia und Georg reagierte Ludwig XV. am 15. Mai 1744 mit einer Kriegserklärung an Großbritannien. Für Hogarth hatte diese Tatsache insofern fatale Konsequenzen, als – wie gehört – drei von ihm in Paris engagierte französische Kupferstecher deswegen nicht für ihn arbeiten konnten. Zudem mag ihm unangenehm aufgestoßen sein, dass just zur Entstehungszeit seiner sechs Bilder Friedrich II., der ihm bereits 1743 den Stecher Schmidt vor der Nase weggeschnappt hatte, sich am 22. Mai 1744 auch noch mit dem britischen Erzfeind Frankreich verbündete.[109] All dies könnte mit ein Grund dafür gewesen sein, dass Hogarth in Szene 4 seiner *Marriage-A-la-Mode*-Serie den Preußenkönig dadurch verunglimpfte, dass er ihn mit deutlich sichtbarer Adlernase vor Michelangelos *Ganymed* einen italienischen Kastraten mit seiner Querflöte begleiten lässt – einen jener entmannten Sänger, für die der Monarch so sehr schwärmte, für die aber der Künstler nur Spott übrig hatte.[110]

Doch ganz unabhängig von solchen Spekulationen ist es höchst bemerkenswert, dass es sich bei Hogarths Repräsentation offenbar um die einzige zeitgenössische Darstellung handelt, die den Alten Fritz als schwul outet. Und dies bereits im Jahre 1744! Kein anderes, öffentlich zirkulierendes Dokument oder Bild tat dies bis dato. Erstaunlich, dass diese Tatsache den zahlreichen Interpreten bis heute verborgen blieb.[111]

---

108 Siehe Hans-Bernd Spies/Helmut Winter (Hrsg.): *Die Schlacht bei Dettingen 1743: Beiträge zum 250. Jahrestag* (Aschaffenburg: Geschichts- und Kunstverein Aschaffenburg e.V. 1993) [*Veröffentlichungen des Geschichts- und Kunstvereins Aschaffenburg e.V., Band 38*]. Vgl. auch das Gemälde von Hogarths Freund John Wootton: *King George II at the Battle of Dettingen, with the Duke of Cumberland and Robert, 4th Earl of Holderness, 27 June 1743* (1743; National Army Museum, London), das Georg zu Pferde als ruhmreichen Sieger in der Schlacht bei Dettingen zeigt. Siehe Andrew C. Thompson: *George II: King and Elector* (New Haven und London: Yale University Press 2011), 153, Abb. 10 und Cover-Illustration.

109 Zu Hogarths Patriotismus und seiner frankophoben Gesinnung: Nichols: *Biographical Anecdotes of William Hogarth*, 42–44, 293–294; Krysmanski: "O the Roast Beef of Old England"; Peter Wagner: "The Artistic Framing of English Nationalism in Hogarth's *The Gate of Calais, or, The Roast Beef of Old England*", in: Frédéric Ogée (Hrsg.): *'Better In France?' The Circulation of Ideas Across the Channel in the Eighteenth Century* (Lewisburg, PA: Bucknell University Press, 2005), 71–87. Erst am 26. August 1745, als die Konvention von Hannover unterzeichnet wurde, schloss Preußen mit Großbritannien wieder Frieden – zu spät für Hogarths *Marriage-A-la-Mode*-Serie. Siehe Uriel Dann: *Hanover and Great Britain, 1740–1760: Diplomacy and Survival* (Leicester, London: Leicester University Press 1991), 69.

110 Hogarth nahm in seinen Werken vor allem die zeitgenössische Schwärmerei für Kastraten und die übertrieben hohen Honorare, die die italienischen Sänger kassierten, aufs Korn. Vgl. auch Barlow: *'The Enraged Musician': Hogarth's Musical Imagery*, 190–195.

111 Schuld daran ist die Geheimniskrämerei des Künstlers, der sich höchst selten zu den Realpersonen äußerte, die seine Bilder so zahlreich bevölkern. Offenbar bereitete es Hogarth ein diebisches Vergnügen, die Betrachter seiner Werke darüber im Unklaren zu lassen, wer alles in seinen Bildern von ihm dargestellt wurde. In vergleichbarer Weise integrierte er zahlreiche schmutzig-obszöne und zweideutig-erotische Mo-

Hinweis:

Eine vom Autor dieser Studie verfasste ausführliche Neuinterpretation aller sechs Szenen von Hogarths *Marriage A-la-Mode* findet sich in einem jüngst erschienenen Essay: „Der pädophile Adelsspross: Warum die arrangierte Ehe ‚nach der Mode' scheitern musste." In: *Lichtenberg-Jahrbuch 2013* (Heidelberg: Universitätsverlag Winter 2015), 57–141. Eine erweiterte englischsprachige Version dieses Essays erscheint – zusammen mit anderen sensationellen Forschungsergebnissen, die 38 Autoren aus 9 Ländern vorlegen – im verspäteten Jubiläumsband *250 Years On: New Light On William Hogarth. 47 Essays to Commemorate the 250th Anniversary of Hogarth's Death* bei Krysman Press.

---

tive, die auf menschliche Geschlechtsteile anspielen, oder versteckte humorige Wortspiele in seine Bildwelt. Siehe Krysmanski: *Hogarth's Hidden Parts*, 120–179, 233–235. Auch pflegte er die zeitgenössischen Kunstkenner über jene Motive in seinen Werken rätseln zu lassen, die er ganz bewusst – mal mehr und mal weniger deutlich – bei den alten Meistern entlehnt hat. Vor allem die Hogarth-Forschung des 20. Jahrhunderts hat sich mit diesem „borrowing"-Konzept, das ich an anderer Stelle als „Anti-Ikonographie" bezeichnet habe, intensiv auseinandergesetzt. Siehe Frederick Antal: "Hogarth and His Borrowings", *The Art Bulletin* 29 (March 1947), 36–48; ders.: *Hogarth and his Place in European Art* (London: Routledge & Kegan Paul 1962); Werner Busch: *Nachahmung als bürgerliches Kunstprinzip: Ikonographische Zitate bei Hogarth und in seiner Nachfolge* (Hildesheim und New York: Georg Olms Verlag 1977); Bernd W. Krysmanski: *Hogarth's 'Enthusiasm Delineated': Nachahmung als Kritik am Kennertum. Eine Werkanalyse. Zugleich ein Einblick in das sarkastisch-aufgeklärte Denken eines "Künstlerrebellen" im englischen 18. Jahrhundert*, 2 Bände (Hildesheim, Zürich, New York: Georg Olms Verlag 1996).

Is the only true likeness of Frederick the Great to be found in Hogarth's *Marriage A-la-Mode?*

(A supplementary English translation)

Frederick the Great's lack of good looks

Frederick the Great disliked his own features. He even considered his own face repulsive when seen in a mirror. Most of his portraits disgusted him. The reason was simple: he was convinced that he was ugly. There is a death mask of him, taken by Johann Eckstein on 17 August 1786, which demonstrates precisely what had led him to this conviction. Old Fritz, as he was nicknamed, had a prominently hooked and aquiline nose, and little else to recommend him to connoisseurs of classical ideals of good looks.

Johann Caspar Lavater, the self-styled expert physiognomist, had examined Frederick the Great's appearance at close quarters, and had categorised him as "not of the handsome type, which painters well-versed in ideal physiognomies venerate—not of that type of magnificence—and decidedly not good-looking." It cannot be doubted that Frederick was well aware of his facial defects. He once remarked to the Marquis d'Argens that "people say that we terrestrial kings are made in the image of God. Then I look in the mirror, and am obliged to say to myself: How unlucky for God!" But he expressed this self-castigation with a bitter sense of humour. Referring to his prominent proboscis, he would say: "My nose may be large, but it's not for dancing around." The older he got, the more he neglected his outward appearance, and the less attention he paid to his personal grooming. "Don't I look a bit of a pig?" he once jokingly asked his reader and private secretary, Henri de Catt.

The idealised portraits

It was however only those of his immediate circle who knew the true appearance of the king's visage. Official portraitists flattered him all too skilfully with the deftness of their brushwork. None of the extant portraits depict Frederick as he really was: in fact, quite the opposite: almost all of them showed the face of the young Prussian king in an all too generalised if not idealised form, i.e. without the aquiline nose, being respectful representations of kingship, perhaps, that is, with the exception of some of his later portraits.

Nor were the coins that were issued around 1740 on the occasion of Frederick's accession to the throne, and those later, any better. Almost all of these representations were more or less free inventions of his appearance, as the king had an aversion to sitting for portraiture. He did not consider himself to be an Apollo, a Mars or an Adonis. He wrote on 14 December 1774 to Jean-Baptiste le Rond d'Alembert: "One has to be Apollo, Mars or Adonis to have oneself painted, and since I do not have the honour of being one of these gentlemen, I have refrained from the brush as much as possible whenever it was up to me." Further in 1743 Frederick responded to his friend Voltaire who had asked him for a recent portrait with this tart rebuff: "I was not painted, and I will no longer let myself be painted. I can only give you medals."

All this was of course being somewhat economical with the truth, because portraits of him did exist, especially as there was a demand for his likeness from all of the courts of Europe. However, such portraits were mostly based on sketches by artists who only roughly recorded the appearance of the king, and then at a distance. In order to flatter their monarch, they provided the young king with smooth facial features and a classically straight nose. This is particularly evident when rendered in full profile, as in a pastel by Georg Wenzeslaus von Knobelsdorff showing the head of the crown prince from the righthand side. Furthermore, once new portraits became available, such as Antoine Pesne's breast-pieces, they were immediately and repeatedly reproduced by lesser hands. Engraved portraits too, for instance by Georg Friedrich Schmidt, Johann Georg Wille, Antoine Benoist and Thomas Burford, which were well known throughout Europe, show the face of the younger monarch also in an idealised form, and of course without a hooked aquiline nose. Comparing these portraits it is hard to believe that they are of the same person, the King of Prussia. Interestingly, Frederick was unhappy even with the portraits commissioned by his relatives. When giving one of them to the Masonic lodge of his nephew, Prince Frederick Augustus of Brunswick Wolfenbüttel, he recommended that the picture should be better used as a scarecrow.

Apart from Antoine Pesne's miniature representation of the 21-year-old crown prince of 1733, the only authorised portrait, for which Frederick allegedly sat for a few hours, is the one painted in 1763 by his court painter, Johann Georg Ziesenis. Yet it is still not certain whether or not the monarch sat for this latter "bourgeois" painting. It was commissioned by Philippine Charlotte of Brunswick-Wolfenbüttel, the sister of the king, and shows his highness without a hooked nose. So this is also a highly idealised portrait, which is why one can hardly speak of it as a credible representation of Frederick himself, as has occasionally been claimed.

After that date, Old Fritz is depicted in a more unconventional way. He is shown, for instance, wearing a rather plain-looking uniform in Johann Heinrich Christian Franke's portrait of 1763/64, where the monarch holds aloft a tricorn hat in his right hand in halfhearted salute. In a gouache of 1772 by Daniel Chodowiecki he is posed rather awkwardly in a slightly bent position on horseback, which a few years later served as a model for an engraving. Last but not least the king is depicted in a popular painting by Anton Graff (Charlottenburg Palace) as a rather kindly ageing sovereign, as observed by the artist while on parade in 1781. The Frederick on horseback from the print version of Johann Heinrich Lips after Chodowiecki was used by Lavater in 1777 as an illustration for his *Physiognomische Fragmente*, because the author was of the opinion that here "the Great, He himself, was riding past", as he was known from life—a representation that drove away all other pictures of Frederick from the author's mind: "[...] So he was [...] (as far as a small representation, the etching needle and the draughtsman's imagination can achieve it!) [...] And not like [the engraver Johann Georg] Wille had splendidly metallised him" on copperplate. Nevertheless, even in Lips's print the nose of the king is portrayed in a more flattering and straightened form. It seems that in Lavater's view the King of Prussia could not conceivably be portrayed with a disfiguring crooked nose.

More realistic portraits, old-age, and Menzel's flute-playing Frederick

Because there was—with the possible exception of the unauthorised later portraits—no truly authentic portrait of Frederick in the eighteenth century that came close to the head of state's actual appearance, Adolph Menzel in the nineteenth century was not able to use an appropriate model for his famous representation of his *Flute Concert of Sanssouci* (1850/52; Nationalgalerie Berlin) that reproduced the face of the King of Prussia as he was in his younger years. So it is hardly surprising that a viewer from today said about the main character in this picture: "That's never Old Fritz, that's Mozart!" Even though it was apparently difficult for this sceptical viewer to believe, it is in fact Menzel's version of a private evening concert of Frederick the Great that is being depicted in the Berlin painting, the monarch's flute-playing celebrated in performance before distinguished guests and in a candlelit atmosphere interpreted to the smallest detail with sensitivity in imitation of the Rococo. Although the Prussian king appears realistically painted, he is transfigured into an idealised form, so that it is quite understandable that the flute player here could be easily confused with Mozart, albeit by this mis-informed observer. Typically however, Menzel, once again, shows Frederick, as if by a matter of course, with a flattering straightened nose.

Hogarth's depiction of the homosexual Frederick

Is there really no unflattering portrait of Frederick, which shows him with a hooked nose as his dominant facial feature? Indeed, such a depiction does exist, however, in a most unexpected place and, what is more, in a satirical context, and it is possibly for this reason the subject has remained undetect-ed for over 270 years. The artist is none other than the English painter and engraver William Hogarth (1697–1764), especially known for his satirical and sarcastic "modern moral subjects". Scene 4 of his famous six-part series *Marriage A-la-Mode* (1743–44; National Gallery, London; engravings 1745) shows a *levée* in the bedroom of the Countess Squander, as was then com-mon among the aristocracy. In it, Frederick the Great appears as a flautist behind a singing Italian castrato and in front of a painting that shows—in imitation of a Michelangelo drawing—a homoerotic scene, namely Jupiter as an eagle abducting the beautiful boy Ganymede, with whom he has madly fallen in love, off to Mount Olympus.

But why should Frederick appear in Hogarth's picture? First of all, it should be noted that the image illustrates a case of adultery: the lady of the house, who is being coiffed, is attentively flirting with her lover, who in turn invites her to an erotic masquerade. Meanwhile, on the other side of the picture, her entirely apathetic husband casually sips a cup of hot chocolate. Because of the curlers in his hair together with the horned Actacon figure lying in a basket among other auction items and to which an oriental boy points with a twinkle in his eye, Hogarth satirically marks out the lady's husband, Lord Squanderfield, as being repeatedly cuckolded. But not only this: Hogarth's arrangement of figures reveals that the guests and hosts of the *levée* scene are divided into two groups with respect to their sexual ori-entations: one half of the picture is reserved for the countess and her lover willingly compliant in heterosexual adultery, to which a painting on the wall alludes that shows Correggio's naked, ecstatic *Io* (*c.*1530; Kunsthistorisches Museum, Vienna) being surreptitiously seduced by Jupiter in the form of a grey amorphous cloud. On the opposite side of the scene we see male repre-sentatives of a very different sexual persuasion that have one thing in com-mon: the love of their own sex or—more disturbingly to the modern view-er—an unwholesome sexual interest in children. To this set the paedophilic lord belongs and is shown as the central character of the group. In order to make clear that he has little interest in husbandly marital sex he is here surrounded exclusively by homosexual references. In the previous scene a bisexual preference shows him with an innocent young girl prostitute, but significantly his true sexual predilections are demonstrated by an auction catalogue that is lying on the floor, which refers to a certain "S[i]r Tim[oth]y Babyhouse". (Surely it is not by coincidence the name "Timothy" was formerly an English usage for a child's penis!) Old Fritz, the flautist, would then be the most prominent among the "sodomites" in the image, whose presences are there to besmirch the lord who is openly cuckolded by his wife because he has little desire to fulfil her sexual needs.

Formally and physically, the portly figure of the singer at the front of this group takes up the most of the space. He is adorned, and feminised, with numerous pieces of jewellery, as revealed by the many rings studded with brilliant stones adorning his fingers and ear. This singer, whom the artist has so clearly marked as a "queen" may be an allusion to Senesino or Carestini or to another Italian castrato that Handel (who, according to some experts, had contacts with homosexuals) had engaged in the 1730s for his Italian operas put on in London. Or could it be that the singer alludes to George Frideric Handel himself? At the time when Hogarth's paintings were executed Handel was almost bankrupt because his Italian operas had flopped and his English oratorios initially had little success in London. This may explain why the artist might have depicted the composer ironically as a singer who was forced by circumstance to participate in providing informal musical performances to small private parties, especially as Handel—which is not widely known—had an ability to sing sweetly. However, if Hogarth had really intended an allusion to Handel himself, it must have been a rather marginal one and then in combination with a ridicule of one of his own castrati.

But is this singer accompanied on the flute by none other than the well-known Frederick II of Prussia? So far, some interpreters are of the opinion that the musician may be Karl Friedrich Weidemann, a flautist and oboist from Handel's opera orchestra, but this assertion is questionable, not least because it is not known whether or not Weidemann had homosexual tendencies. After all, this misinterpretation shows that it must have been common knowledge at the time that the flautist depicted by Hogarth was in fact German.

It is very interesting that the musician, who has raised his flute in the countess's bedroom, is not only connected to the castrato in front of him, but also to a *Ganymede* picture hanging on the wall behind him. And not only that: the eagle in the *Ganymede* picture is depicted seizing his victim from behind, thereby violently spreading out Ganymede's legs with its claws in order to place its tail feathers between the legs of the young man—certainly a coded reference to anal homosexual sex. Furthermore, Hogarth shows the beak of the eagle approaching Ganymede's genitals in a menacing manner, as if the young man is threatened with castration, should he resist. And this picture, of all things, is directly assigned to the flautist, who also has a matching aquiline nose and plays upon a phallic symbol, the flute, blowing if not kissing it with his lips.

Was Old Fritz really gay?

Frederick the Great played the German flute excellently, he composed 121 sonatas for the instrument and practiced it for at least four times a day, considering the musical activity an escape from his onerous state duties. It is further known that he had had homosexual tendencies and became infatuated with Italian castrati. The monarch even took his favourite singers with him while travelling abroad. Enthusiastically, he announced to his friend Count Friedrich Rudolf von Rothenburg: "My Italian castrati are on the way. It is said that they are of a particular caliber and—as well as they sing—they will turn the heads of all in Berlin." On 12 December 1743 the castrato Felice Salimbeni, who possessed a vocal range of two and a half octaves and whom the monarch considered the best of all Italian singers, arrived in Berlin.

It should not be surprising to the Prussian king's contemporaries if they were of the opinion that such an enthusiasm could only come about because of Frederick's homosexual preferences. The young crown prince was already denigrated by his father, the "Soldier King" Frederick William I, as a "sodomite" and an effeminate good-for-nothing, devoid of "appropriate" male inclination, who styled his hair like a fool, grimaced with his face, and only showed interest for distracting divers amusements. Frederick himself admitted to his mentor, General Field Marshal Friedrich Wilhelm von Grumbkow, that he felt less attracted to women, and, in contrast, he had a penchant for attractive young pages and the *Lange Kerls* ("tall boys") of the Grand Grenadiers of Potsdam, also known as the Potsdam Giants. The cuirassier lieutenant Hans Hermann von Katte, his boyfriend, with whom he wanted to elope, was sentenced to death by Frederick's father as an example against the "sodomitical" impulses of his son—certainly a very traumatic experience for the young prince who was well aware of his deepening homosexual leanings. Peter Karl Christoph von Keith, a page of the crown prince, was from a young age also one of Frederick's intimates and a participant in his acts of supposed sexual deviation. Furthermore, the young king seems to have had a long-standing homosexual relationship with his valet and companion, Michael Gabriel Fredersdorf, and he was envious of the lovers of his brother Henry who lived openly as a homosexual. Frederick wrote about a very attractive page that both brothers equally adored: "You must love him if you see him, and worship, if you know him." (Some intimate letters that express their opinions on such liaisons still remain unpublished and are held in the Secret State Archives in Berlin.)

It is no wonder, therefore, that in 1772 Johann Georg Hamann insulted the King of Prussia, with reference to him in terms of anal intercourse by calling him *Aftokrator* (instead of autokrator) and in identifying several men in his circle as "warm brothers". Voltaire was one of the first to make widely known the sexual proclivities of the Prussian monarch. He used to call Frederick in back slang, *Luc*. Read in reverse, it says *cul*—the French term for the human rump. He described the sex life of the king as follows:

> Once booted and dressed, His Majesty's Stoic proclivities would cause him to devote a short spell to the cult of Epicurus. Two or three favourites would be summoned; lieutenants from his regiment, or pages, or haidouks, or young cadets. They would take coffee together, and then the one favoured with the handkerchief would stay another fifteen minutes, for a twosome. Matters never progressed to the ultimate, given that, while his father had still been alive, the Prince had been caused severe suffering on account of his passing fancies; and his wounds had never really healed. Unable to play the major role, he had to settle for a secondary part.

In a similar vein, Baron von Diebitsch related that his majesty allowed "several of his favourites" to take part in the said ritual of taking coffee, both in the morning and in the afternoon, among them a page called von Sydow. In his memoirs, Casanova confirms the more passive role that the frail Frederick, according to Voltaire, played in his same-sex affairs: every soldier of the First Potsdam Battalion "had a gold watch in the fob of his breeches. It was thus that the king rewarded the courage with which they had subjugated him as Caesar subjugated Nicomedes in Bithynia. No secret was made of it."

Nor was the monarch's art-loving passion for collecting unaffected by his homosexual preferences. In 1747 the famous ancient bronze of the *Praying Boy*, which was then believed to be a representation of Antinous, was acquired by Frederick most likely for its overt eroticism and he had it erected in

Sanssouci. Furthermore, the well-known Berlin Enlightenment writer, book-seller and chronicler Friedrich Nicolai reported that the king had acquired through the art dealer Jacques Trible an Indian ink drawing by Giulio Roma-no showing a "Priapeia".

Nicolai also gave further accounts that Frederick spontaneously commis-sioned "lewd" paintings in order to play all kinds of practical jokes on his guests at Potsdam Castle. For instance, when the king heard that the old Duke of Hollstein-Beck had asked for "female company", he quickly let a "very ordinary painter do a little painting of a satyr with a nymph, not quite a foot high, with a green curtain in front of it, and had it secretly hung in the room of the Duke". On another occasion, when the Duke-Bishop of Breslau was staying in the same room, the king ordered to have another painting, this time showing a monk and a nun copulating, then have it hung in the room. During his "round table" gatherings, where Frederick's close friend Francesco Algarotti participated and which were usually approached infor-mally and cheerfully and without conforming to prescribed etiquette, the monarch was prone to making openly disambiguous narratives, especially if women were not present (as was often the case). His physician Johann Georg von Zimmermann says that Frederick, during such occasions, more than once told a risqué story about Emperor Leopold, who had suffered from high fever: at the request of his personal physician the Emperor was retired to a hermetically sealed, completely darkened room. But in the pitch-black-ness the doctor had trouble in finding the bed of the monarch.

> Finally he succeeded. But now the personal physician was in great need of how and where he should find the arm of the Emperor in order to feel his pulse. He touched, very slowly, the blanket, the bed, and the Emper-or, with whom he could not [according to convention] talk because he was a very reticent and dignified man. At last he was successful and the doctor believed that he had finally found the arm of the Emperor. So he counted attentively, with squinted face, the pulse. But the Emperor, sur-prised at this outrageous blunder, pointed out the stupid doctor's error with utmost dignity by pathetically, thoughtfully and slowly telling this Esculap: *hoc est membrum nostrum imperial sacro-caesareum.*

Such ribald and obscene jokes suggest that Frederick II was not prudish and must have been open-minded with regards to his sexual desires. Indeed, one is inclined to believe that he was unconcerned about such matters, and neither was he furtive about his sexuality nor did he suppress it in favour of an asexual life, as has been claimed by some historians. It is no wonder, then, that the known homosexual classicist, Johann Joachim Winckelmann, enjoyed himself immensely because of the "Greek taste in love" that prevailed at Frederick's court. In a letter dated 27 March 1752 to his friend Hieronymus Dietrich Berendis he wrote enthusiastically about his visit to Sanssouci: "I have enjoyed lusts, the likes of which I will not enjoy again: I saw Athens and Sparta in Potsdam and I am filled with worshipful admiration for the divine monarch."

There can be no doubt that a surprisingly large number of contemporaries were conversant with the Prussian king's homosexual leanings, although the term used today for same-sex relationships did not exist in his time. Notwithstanding, von Zimmermann, in a specially written chapter on "Frederick's allegedly Greek taste in love" in his fragments on Frederick the Great, tried to preserve the honour of his monarch by claiming that the crown prince had had no aversion to female company before his sham marriage to Elisabeth Christine of Brunswick-Wolfenbüttel, but shortly before his wedding suffered from a sexually transmitted disease caught while frequenting prostitutes. To stop the extremely violent venereal spermatorrhea, he had put himself into the hands of a quack whose mistreatment called for a radical corrective surgery six months later, resulting in a cruel cut. This, however, would have mutilated the monarch so that he considered himself to be impotent and no longer dared to undress in front of others or to sleep with his wife. For Oliver Das Gupta, the calculation of von Zimmermann's fictitious story is clear: "A Teutonic hero had neither to be asexual nor gay, but such an idol could well suffer from venereal disease." So Wolfgang Burgdorf is probably right in thinking that "Frederick had a physical disgust of women", so much so that "he was unable to sleep with them". Above all, the many contemporary voices cannot be simply swept away, as even von Zimmermann frankly quoted them:

> Frederick lost a great deal of "sensual pleasure", says Mr. Büsching, a Prussian ecclesiastic counsellor, "by his aversion to women; but he indemnified himself by his intercourse with men, recollecting from the history of philosophy, that Socrates was reported to have been very fond of Alcibiades". Not only Mr. Büsching, however, but also Voltaire, la Beaumelle, the Duke de Choiseul, innumerable Frenchmen and Germans, almost all the friends and enemies of Frederick, almost all the princes and great men of Europe, even his servants—even the confidants and friends of his later years, were of the opinion that he had loved, as it is pretended, Socrates loved Alcibiades.

Clear words indeed! The king himself was the author of the comic, frivolously blasphemous mock-heroic poem *Le Palladion* (1749), which does not spare allusions to activity below the waistline and in which several homosexual practices are explicitly described. In it we find not only mentioned famous homosexuals from Alcibiades to Caesar, but also the following blasphemous lines:

> Ce bon Saint Jean, que pensez-vous qu'il fit,
> Pour que Jésus le couchât sur son lit?
> Sentez-vous pas qu'il sut son Ganymède.
> (The good Saint John, what do you think he did,
> To induce Jesus to sleep with him in his bed?
> And don't you feel that he knew his Ganymede.)

In this respect, the flute-playing King of Prussia fits in quite well with the *Ganymede* painting and the other homosexuals in Hogarth's picture, including a man who effeminately waves out to the viewer and from whose limp wrist dangles a fan.

That the Ganymede myth seems to entirely fit the monarch's sexual taste is proven by the fact that the ceiling paintings for the Marble Hall of the Potsdam New Palace, which were finished in 1768, show Ganymede being brought to Olympus and passed through Hebe, the goddess of youth, to Jupiter's table. But when the king took a closer look at the painting by Charles-Amédée Philippe van Loo he discovered his initials on a tablet carried by some genii of fame behind Jupiter. Indignant, he ordered the erasure of these letters. Did it, one wonders, embarrass him that his name was brought into direct connection with Ganymede? And was this because Frederick also knew of Hogarth's engraving series known about in Prussia, *Marriage A-la-Mode*, which had been published in 1745, and had recognised himself as the flautist positioned in front of the Ganymede image?

How did Hogarth know of Frederick's aquiline nose?

Hogarth obviously knew a lot about the sexual preferences of the Prussian king. But how could he, at the time of the painting's execution in 1743–44, have been informed about Old Fritz's hooked nose, as the death mask of the monarch so impressively demonstrates? Certainly not through the idealised portraits that were widespread at the time. Maybe it was through contacts with British aristocrats or with people in Voltaire's circle, as some of them may have met Frederick personally? And not only through these channels: during his stay in Paris in May and June 1743, the artist had the opportunity to acquaint himself with the features of the Prussian king. When looking for French engravers for his planned engravings of *Marriage A-la-Mode*, he visited the studios of many artists of the *Académie Royale*, including Georg Friedrich Schmidt (1712–1775), who had acquired something of a reputation as an outstanding engraver in the French capital because of his soft and fine lines. Significantly, Schmidt, in 1743, had worked on a new portrait of Frederick the Great.

This German engraver and etcher was initially educated in Berlin, where he made friends with the court painter Antoine Pesne, who had worked at the Prussian court from 1711 and stood "in an intimate, personal relation" with Frederick the Great. In Berlin Schmidt had engraved portraits of the crown prince, who was coincidentally the same age as the engraver. However, in 1737 he left, with a letter of recommendation by Pesne, for Paris. There he refined his Rococo style to perfection. He was so successful in Paris that in 1742, despite his being a Protestant, he was admitted through the express auspices of the French king, Louis XV, to the *Académie Royale*. It is therefore more than likely Hogarth tried to hire this emerging German artist—along with other French engravers—to execute the engraved version of his *Marriage A-la-Mode* series. If for this reason alone, Hogarth must have visited Schmidt in his studio where he must have seen the engraver's current work, especially the 1743 portrait of Frederick the Great. Perhaps Hogarth learned from Schmidt that he executed the face of the monarch in a highly idealised form according to the prevailing conventions of portraiture, and that the Prussian king in fact looked more hard-featured and had a distinctive aquiline nose. Most probably Hogarth had also the opportunity to see more realistic sketches of Frederick's visage there.

Ludwig D. Jacoby writes about Schmidt: "Among his excellent talents was also that he could draw correctly after nature, which does not always happen with the most skilled engravers." In this respect, one may assume that Schmidt was able to capture all of the characteristic facial features of a person with his drawing skills—as Hogarth, who is still famous for his depiction of characters, was equally able to do—and was well gifted to correctly depict the physiognomy of Frederick, even if no such drawings have survived. The question, of course, is whether the German artist personally contacted the Prussian King in 1743 in order to make some sketches of him for his current portrait. In fact, the name "Schmidt" did appear in Frederick's *Schatullrechnungen* (a payment book from his privy purse) for May 1743. So it is conceivable that Schmidt visited the monarch, but that the king did not, as usual, oblige the artist with any sittings. This, however, may not have prevented him from making some fresh sketches, especially as he was known to frequently practice drawing. In addition, Schmidt knew the crown prince from his early Berlin years, so that he might have shown Hogarth by means of some sketches—even from memory—Frederick's prominent nose.

Schmidt may also have informed Hogarth about the homosexual tendencies of the Prussian king, which he must have known about; even if not firsthand, yet more than might be supposed. The mere fact that Schmidt was born on the same day as the crown prince and had met him at a young age suggests that there probably was, from the beginning, a relatively intimate relationship between the two men. From 1730 to 1736 Schmidt completed his Prussian military service, which, however, had been reduced (perhaps at the instigation of Frederick?) through the intercession of Field Marshal von Grumbkow from fourteen to six years, so that he could focus increasingly on his artistic studies. Furthermore, he had a lifelong friendship with Georg Wenzeslaus von Knobelsdorff, who originally was also a soldier and had studied with Schmidt at the Berlin Academy of Art. And as the head custodian of royal buildings von Knobelsdorff belonged to the inner circle of men around Frederick. After his departure to Paris, Schmidt was for a while financially supported by the Prussian king. In the French capital he stayed for several years as a roommate with his fellow artist and friend, Johann Georg Wille, where they lived a youthful bibulous life. Probably they shared a sexually intimate friendship. Occasional remarks in letters suggest that Wille had "been closer to [Schmidt]" than one would assume. Furthermore, Schmidt married his wife, Dorothee Luise Videbant, in 1746 primarily because of a high dowry and had no qualms about leaving his wife and son for a long period, when in 1757 he left for St. Petersburg for a few years.

So it is quite possible that Schmidt even had a sexual relationship with Frederick II, who, with the participation of von Knobelsdorff, called the engraver back to Berlin, though there is no concrete evidence for such a relationship. Or is there? In a letter to Goethe, Carl Friedrich Zelter wrote about his great-uncle Schmidt that "morally he was of the same disposition as his king, which wasn't then held in high esteem". Does Zelter here say with paraphrastic words that both men shared the same sexual preferences? Perhaps these were well known in Zelter's family. Then it should not be excluded that the young Schmidt had been one of the "favourites" of the Prussian crown prince. Anyway, there is some evidence that Hogarth owes his information about Frederick's sexual orientation to Schmidt, when he visited him in Paris in order to hire him for the execution of at least one of the engravings of his *Marriage A-la-Mode* series.

That Hogarth must have appeared in Schmidt's studio is proved by an advertisement in the *Daily Advertiser* of 8 November 1744. There it is mentioned that in June 1743 Bernard Baron, Simon François Ravenet, Louis Gérard Scotin, Jacques Philippe Le Bas, an engraver named Dupré (probably a confusion with Nicolas Gabriel Dupuis) and "Suberan" (i.e. Pierre Soubeyran, one of Schmidt's students!) had agreed to work for Hogarth, each of them willing to execute one plate of his six-part series. However, because of the war with France, the three latter engravers could not comply with the commitment because they were unable to leave Paris for London, which is why the completion of the engravings was delayed for several months. Significantly in his advertisement Hogarth mentioned Schmidt's student Soubeyran by name. So he must have visited the Paris studio of the German master in 1743. At such a time he must surely have talked with Schmidt about his current portrait of Frederick the Great and Hogarth's plan to let the *Marriage A-la-Mode* series be engraved by Parisian artists. Additionally, because of their similar ribald humour, Schmidt and Hogarth would have had a splendid opportunity to share social chitchat and to understand one-another, and to have had a great time together in Paris. Since both appreciated the boozy tavern life, it is to be assumed that the English artist, during their clashing of glasses, could easily have elicited from his German soulmate some of the more saucy details of the Prussian king's goings-on. That Hogarth must have been able to communicate with Schmidt in French can be seen from his handwritten translation of Claude-Henri Watelet's *L'art de peindre* (1760).

The artist was probably upset with the King of Prussia

However, Schmidt did not commit himself to engrave any of the *Marriage A-la-Mode* pictures, as at that time he was being encouraged to return home to Berlin by Frederick. On 6 July 1743 a certificate was issued appointing Schmidt as court engraver to the Prussian king, offering the German artist a generous salary of 600 talers; this, after some hesitation and much French pressure to keep him in Paris, Schmidt eventually agreed to and returned to Berlin. Perhaps Schmidt had initially promised to work for Hogarth, but was later enticed by Frederick's more lucrative offer. This solicitation would also explain why Hogarth was cross with the King of Prussia and with a pique of annoyance depicted him in the *Levée* scene of his *Marriage A-la-Mode* series as a kind of counterpart to the idealised portrait by Schmidt, namely by portraying him as a paederastic flautist and a little older than he actually was, in much the same way as using an age progression tool of computer face-aging software, which is able to show people their "future face", decade by decade, as they grow older.

It is known that in comparable situations the English artist similarly and testily responded and tended to denigrate contemporaries with his brush and burin, if they were not acting in his best interests, or if he didn't like them for any other reason. On the other hand, Hogarth's pictures abound with representations of popular contemporaries or persons from his immediate circle, these being obviously added for his personal amusement in his character-rich scenes. It is as if he wished to encourage the viewer to search for such familiar faces in his works. What is more, he seems to have been able to represent the facial features of his contemporaries older than they really were. His treatise, *The Analysis of Beauty* (1753) indicates that Hogarth knew how the human face changes over a life-span so that he could easily envisage the future look of Frederick the Great. In the chapter "Of the Face" the artist shows "in what manner the lines of the face alter from infancy upwards, and specify the different ages". He emphasises that in "the age from twenty to thirty [...] there appears but little change". However, "after this time, as the alterations grow more and more visible, we perceive the sweet simplicity of many rounding parts of the face, begin to break into dented shapes, with more sudden turns about the muscles, occasioned by their many repeated movements [...]" And finally, after the age of fifty or so, more strokes and cuts were to be laid on and "those lineaments that have once been elegant, retain their flowing turns in venerable age, leaving to the last a comely piece of ruin". So Hogarth may have deliberately shown the Prussian king older and somewhat in caricature. It is also possible that in his younger years Frederick may have looked quite old, so that Hogarth might have depicted the actual features of the Prussian king much better than Schmidt in his youthful looking, unrealistically flattering portrait.

Moreover, could it be, not only Frederick II, but also his newly engaged court-engraver was taken up as a homosexual in Hogarth's picture? Is it possible that the effeminate man with the fan dangling from his wrist waving from behind at the castrato is a caricature of Schmidt? Comparing Hogarth's depiction of a gay man with Schmidt's *Self Portrait with a Spider in the Window*, which was etched in 1758 in the style of Rembrandt, we can, after all, find the following matches: the round face; the relatively narrow mouth with full lips; a similar nose shape; and clearly visible dark circles about the eyes, these details thereby being satirically overaccentuated by Hogarth in order to underline the womanly features in a man. It may be not by chance that both figures wear similar-looking white frilled shirts that are tightly closed about the neck. Also noteworthy are the expressive hands shown in Schmidt's self-portrait, stressing how important they are for the artist. Hogarth also lays emphasis on the hands, but ironically underscores the feminine waving gesture, which is used to initiate same-sex contacts. Had Schmidt made no secret of his sexual orientation, one wonders, so that in Hogarth's engraving he was blatantly presented to the viewer as openly gay?

If the waving man, who additionally wears a beauty spot on the lower lip and whose nose appears slightly deformed by syphilis, is in fact Schmidt, then Hogarth would not only have clearly marked him out as a promiscuous homosexual, but he would also be the ideal adjunct figure for the flute-playing Old Fritz.

Be that as it may, the wig worn by the flautist is similar to the one worn by the younger Frederick in Schmidt's portrait. That it looks greyer than the other wigs may be due to the fact that the fashionably negligent Frederick wore a wig with queue, the lack of care of which was all too visible. The simple clothing of the flute player could, in addition, allude to the known fact that the monarch was usually informally dressed. Even if we suppose that in Hogarth's depiction the flute-playing Frederick was given his significant aquiline nose to establish a direct connection to the eagle beak in the *Ganymede* image, one could well come to the conclusion that the Prussian king's features are in scene 4 of *Marriage A-la-Mode* much more realistically represented than all other portraits of him. Let us not forget that, in this connection, a crowned black eagle was for centuries the imposing emblem of the Kingdom of Prussia—an eagle as it also appears in Schmidt's 1743 portrait of Frederick.

Crébillon's "Le Sopha"—a reference to Old Fritz

In scene 4 of *Marriage A-la-Mode* an erotic book, *Le Sopha*, lies on the sofa. It is said to have been commissioned by the King of Prussia and may therefore be an additional, hidden clue to the viewer that it is in fact Frederick who is being depicted in the scene. This parody of the *Tales from a Thousand and One Nights* was written by Claude Prosper de Jolyot Crébillon and published in 1742. In the same year it was translated into English as *The Sofa: A Moral Tale*. It relates the experiences of the soul of the voluptuary Amanzéi, condemned by the god Brahma to dwell within a sofa only to be freed if a truly innocent couple experience their first true act of fulfilled love-making on "his" sofa. But, as in all good stories, it takes a while for this to happen, and the sofa in which Amanzéi's soul was imprisoned experiences lots of lewdly lascivious behaviour. That this book emerges as a secondary motif in Hogarth's picture cannot be a coincidence. Yet another supporting point as to the identity of the figure in Hogarth's scheme as being "Old Fritz" may be proffered here: who else would be better placed with a flute between the paederastically suggestive picture of an eagle and one of his beloved castrati singing in front of it?

Frederick also appears in other works by Hogarth

That the artist took an interest in the Prussian monarch on other occasions is proven by the ironic dedication to him below the engraved version of his *March to Finchley* (1750/51). It reads: "To His MAJESTY the KING of PRUS[S]IA, an Encourager of ARTS and SCIENCES! This Plate is most Humbly Dedicated." In the painting of the same title (Foundling Museum, London), which was executed about one year earlier, Hogarth recalled the Scottish threat of the years 1745–46, against which the Grenadier Guards—some still drunk, some cooing with their sweethearts, some urinating or otherwise engaged—are mustered for a march north to confront the rebellious Jacobites. In the background the ramshackle soldiers are shown marching out under the leadership of the Duke of Cumberland to defeat the Catholic young pretender, Charles Edward Stuart, in the Battle of Culloden. Centrally located in the tumult depicted by Hogarth is a soldier, who like a "Hercules at the Crossroads" must make his decision between as to which suitor to choose: a patriotic but pregnant girl or a wizened Catholic crone. The relative disorder in the foreground may be compared with that in Rembrandt's *Night Watch* (1642; Rijksmuseum, Amsterdam). Such a disparaging depiction of disarray put the militarist-minded King George II, to which the print was originally tended to be dedicated, in a sour mood, especially since he was an art philistine who took little interest in "bainting" and "boetry". George, who was accustomed to a strict Hanoverian military discipline, allegedly complained that the disorderly bustle on the canvas mocked his guardsmen, and therefore refused to have his name associated with the dedication. This is why Hogarth ironically dedicated the print, which was executed by Luke Sullivan, to Frederick the Great, a true patron of the arts.

More than ten years later, in the foreground of his engraving, *The Times*, Plate 1 (1762)—a propagandistic print attacking the supporters of the Seven Years' War as incendiaries who set the world ablaze—Hogarth shows Frederick the Great as a fiddler, once more characteristically portraying him with a prominent nose. He sits, wearing a tricorn hat, like an impoverished street musician between desperate women and children fleeing their war-ravaged homes with their few personal belongings. Perhaps this detail alludes to the fact that in the final stages of the Seven Years' War the Earl of Bute, a close confidant of King George III, refused to give further monetary aid to Prussia, which was in alliance with Britain at that time, thus compelling Frederick II, who on the Continent fought against France, Austria and Russia, into peace talks. In this unfortunate situation the Prussian king seems to have found solace in his music, fiddling as it were while all around him burns.

It is interesting that the ironic dedication under the *March to Finchley* highlights Old Fritz as a patron of the arts and sciences, and that in *The Times*, Plate I, the violinist emphasises the Prussian king's love of music even in difficult circumstances, fiddling while the world goes up in smoke. So it is more than plausible that Hogarth, in the fourth scene of his *Marriage A-la-Mode* series, had already conceived of satirically placing the royal flautist among the other homosexuals who flank the cuckolded, paedophilic lord, in order mockingly to point out the deviant sexual behaviour that was unabashedly and uninhibitedly enjoyed to the full in the higher echelons of society. Moreover, Frederick II was certainly the most prominent gay man of his time, and was therefore surely predestined to appear in an image that denounced such perceived behavioural weakness of the upper classes.

What is it that makes Hogarth's representation so special?

It is very likely that Hogarth's representation is the most realistic depiction of the Prussian king that was ever painted or engraved by any artist. As has been demonstrated above, most other portraits show Frederick's face not in a natural looking way, but in an all too idealised form. This corresponds with the conventions of the time, which differentiated between notions of the body politic (*corpus politicum*) and the body natural or mortal (*corpus naturale*), i.e. between the king in office as head of state—a God-given role— who had to be depicted in an idealised, unrealistic and elevated way, distinct from his mortal body in its real, very human, appearance. In this way, Frauke Mankartz is of the opinion that Frederick could escape representations of his *corpus naturale*, but otherwise fulfilled his "royal ceremonial duties" in so far that he made available his "political body [...] for official portraits", thereby being well aware that these pictures differed greatly from his "natural body". He therefore freely and generously gave to diplomats, and other high-ranking personalities, preciously decorated boxes with his portrait and later statuettes in porcelain or bronze depicting him on horseback. Apparently it bothered no one that in such representational images, which circulated widely in much the same way as today's corporate gifts and merchandise items do, Old Fritz looked very differently from his everyday appearance.

For Hogarth, who was interested in the real physiognomies of his fellow men and who subtly differentiated between characters and caricatures, the old distinction between the glorified body politic and the actual personage of the monarch, the former responsible for the production of idealised portraits, was no longer valid. As for Hogarth, only the real faces of his contemporaries counted, not their idealised image. In this respect, he made no exception when depicting Frederick the Great as ugly as he looked. Or did he even make the king's face a touch uglier, since he had good reason to be angry at him?

One may additionally speculate whether the Prussian king was included in Hogarth's picture also for current political reasons. At the time of the execution of the six *Marriage A-la-Mode* paintings (1743/44) the situation on the Continent between the First and Second Silesian Wars was confusing. Political alliances were in state of constant change. Frederick the Great was in armed conflict especially with Austria. On 23 September 1743, Maria Theresa allied with Britain, which forced the Prussian king to look for new allies. One such ally he found in France, of all countries, against which George II had earlier fought. Through good providence King George, on 27 June 1743, had defeated the French with his British-Hanoverian troops in the Battle of Dettingen—a victory that was greatly celebrated in Britain. But the treaty between Maria Theresa and George II resulted in Louis XV of France declaring war against Great Britain on 15 May 1744. For Hogarth this had an unforeseen consequence in so far as three Parisian engravers he had employed could not fulfil their contractual agreements with him. Additionally, it may have piqued his ire that just at the time of the execution of his six *Marriage A-la-Mode* pictures, Frederick II, who had in 1743 snatched the engraver Schmidt away from him, now, on 22 May 1744, had allied with Britain's archenemy France. Such events might have been the underlying reason for Hogarth to cruelly denigrate the Prussian king in scene 4 of his series by letting him appear with a clearly exaggerated aquiline nose in front of Michelangelo's *Ganymede* and accompanying with his flute an effeminate Italian castrato, for whom the monarch had much admiration and desire, but for whom the artist had only scorn and utter contempt.

But apart from such speculations, it is quite remarkable that Hogarth's depiction of Frederick the Great in this scene apparently is the only truthful contemporary representation of Old Fritz that outed the Prussian king as being gay, and this as early as 1744! No other public document or picture has done this. It is amazing that this has remained hidden to scholars and interpreters of Hogarth's work until now.

Abbildungsverzeichnis

1 Skulptur nach der Totenmaske Friedrichs des Großen (1786; Staatliche Museen zu Berlin – Preußischer Kulturbesitz, Skulpturensammlung). Profilansicht.

2 Antoine Pesne: *Kronprinz Friedrich von Preußen* (1736; Burg Hohenzollern). Öl auf Leinwand. 143 × 113 cm.

3 Antoine Pesne: *Friedrich II. als Kronprinz* (1738; Stiftung Preußische Schlösser und Gärten, Berlin-Brandenburg). Öl auf Leinwand. 80,5 × 65 cm.

4 Antoine Pesne: *Friedrich der Große* (1745; Stiftung Preußische Schlösser und Gärten, Berlin-Brandenburg). Öl auf Leinwand. 81 × 65,5 cm.

5 Antoine Pesne: *Friedrich der Große* (1746; Stiftung Preußische Schlösser und Gärten, Berlin-Brandenburg). Öl auf Leinwand. 220 × 139 cm.

6 Georg Wenzeslaus von Knobelsdorff: *Kronprinz Friedrich* (um 1737; Stiftung Preußische Schlösser und Gärten, Berlin-Brandenburg). Pastell.

7 *Fredericus Borussorum Rex*. Medaille auf die Siege des Jahres 1757. Vorderseite.

8 Thomas Burford: *Frederick II., King of Prussia*. Undatierter Kupferstich.

9 Antoine Benoist: *Frederick III^d, King of Prussia*. Undatierter Kupferstich.

10 Johann Georg Ziesenis: *Friedrich der Große* (1763; ehemals Schloss Monbijou, Berlin). Öl auf Leinwand. 129 × 96 cm. Ausschnitt.

11 Johann Heinrich Christian Franke: *Friedrich II., den Hut ziehend* (1763/64; Stiftung Preußische Schlösser und Gärten, Berlin-Brandenburg). Öl auf Leinwand. 126,5 × 94 cm.

12 Johann Heinrich Lips nach Daniel Chodowiecki: *Friedrich, der König von Preußen, zu Pferde* (1777). Radierung. 22,5 × 19 cm. Ausschnitt.

13 Anton Graff: *Friedrich der Große* (1781; Schloss Charlottenburg). Öl auf Leinwand. 62 × 51 cm.

14 Adolph Menzel: *Das Flötenkonzert in Sanssouci* (1850/52). Öl auf Leinwand. 142 × 305 cm. Ausschnitt.

15 Simon François Ravenet nach William Hogarth: *Marriage A-la-Mode*, Plate 4 (1745). Kupferstich und Radierung. Ausschnitt: Flötenspieler.

16 Simon François Ravenet nach William Hogarth: *Marriage A-la-Mode*, Plate 4 (1745). Kupferstich und Radierung. Ausschnitt: gehörnter Lord.

17 Simon François Ravenet nach William Hogarth: *Marriage A-la-Mode*, Plate 4 (1745). Kupferstich und Radierung. Ausschnitt: Auktionskatalog.

18 Simon François Ravenet nach William Hogarth: *Marriage A-la-Mode*, Plate 4 (1745). Kupferstich und Radierung. 38,3 × 46,5 cm. Gesamtansicht.

19 Balthasar Denner: *Georg Friedrich Händel* (ca. 1726–28; National Portrait Gallery, London). Öl auf Leinwand. 74,9 × 62,6 cm.

20 Joseph Goupy: *The Charming Brute* (1754). Karikatur auf Georg Friedrich Händel. Radierung. 34,5 × 24,3 cm. Kolorierte Fassung.

21 William Hogarth: *Marriage A-la-Mode*, Bild 4: Das Lever (1743/44; National Gallery, London). Öl auf Leinwand. 70 × 90,5 cm. Detail: Musiker.

22 Nicolas Beatrizet nach Michelangelo: *Der Raub des Ganymed* (1542). Kupferstich. 42,5 × 27,8 cm. Ausschnitt: obere Bildhälfte.

23 Simon François Ravenet nach William Hogarth: *Marriage A-la-Mode*, Plate 4 (1745). Kupferstich und Radierung. Ausschnitt: Raub des Ganymed.

24 Simon François Ravenet nach William Hogarth: *Marriage A-la-Mode*, Plate 4 (1745). Kupferstich und Radierung. Ausschnitt: Kopf des Flötenspielers.

25 Skulptur nach der Totenmaske Friedrichs des Großen (1786; Staatliche Museen zu Berlin – Preußischer Kulturbesitz, Skulpturensammlung). Dreiviertelprofil.

26 Georg Friedrich Schmidt: *Fridericus III. Rex Borussiae* (1743). Kupferstich und Radierung. 24 × 17, 2 cm.

27 Simon François Ravenet nach William Hogarth: *Marriage A-la-Mode*, Plate 4 (1745). Ausschnitt. Homosexueller

28 Georg Friedrich Schmidt: *Selbstbildnis „mit der Spinne"* (1758). Radierung. 23,3 × 17,7 cm.

29 Simon François Ravenet nach William Hogarth: *Marriage A-la-Mode*, Plate 4 (1745). Kupferstich und Radierung. Ausschnitt: Der Liebhaber der Gräfin auf dem Sofa.

30 Luke Sullivan nach William Hogarth: *The March to Finchley* (1750/51). Kupferstich und Radierung. 44,4 × 55,8 cm.

31 William Hogarth: *The Times*, Plate 1 (1762). Kupferstich und Radierung. 24,5 × 30,6 cm.

32 William Hogarth: *The Times*, Plate 1 (1762). Kupferstich und Radierung. Ausschnitt: Friedrich der Große.

Literatur

Kirsten Ahrens: *Georg Friedrich Schmidt: Selbstbildnis mit der Spinne*. Aus dem Bestand des Porträtarchivs Diepenbroick im Westfälischen Landesmuseum für Kunst und Kulturgeschichte [*Das Kunstwerk des Monats*/Westfälisches Landesmuseum für Kunst und Kulturgeschichte Münster, Landschaftsverband Westfalen-Lippe, Oktober 1990].

Reinhard Alings: " 'Don't ask – don't tell' – War Friedrich schwul?" In: *Friederisiko: Friedrich der Große*, Ausst.-Kat., Stiftung Preußische Schlösser und Gärten Berlin-Brandenburg im Neuen Palais und Park Sanssouci, 28. April–28. Oktober 2012, 2 Bände (München: Hirmer 2012), Band I: *Die Ausstellung*, 238–247.

William Allan: "Fridericus Rex: The Image of a King", *The Connoisseur* 195 (1977), 42–51.

Frederick Antal: "Hogarth and His Borrowings", *The Art Bulletin* 29 (March 1947), 36–48.

Frederick Antal: *Hogarth and his Place in European Art* (London: Routledge & Kegan Paul 1962).

Aloys Apell: *Das Werk von Georg Friedrich Schmidt, Zeichner, Kupferstecher und Radirer, Schüler von G. P. Busch und Nicolaus de Larmessin, geboren zu Berlin am 24. Januar 1712, arbeitete zu Paris, St. Petersburg und Berlin, woselbst er am 25. Januar 1775 starb* (Dresden: Claus 1886).

Karl Otmar von Aretin: *Friedrich der Große: Größe und Grenzen des Preußenkönigs. Bilder und Gegenbilder* (Freiburg im Breisgau: Herder 1985).

Karl Arndt: " '... anschauende Kenntnis des Menschen in allen Ständen ...': Georg Christoph Lichtenberg als Dolmetsch von William Hogarth". In: Martina Dillmann/Claude Keisch (Hrsg.): *'Marriage A-la-Mode' – Hogarth und seine deutschen Bewunderer*, Ausst.-Kat., Staatliche Museen zu Berlin, Nationalgalerie – Altes Museum, Berlin, 18. Dezember 1998–28. Februar 1999, Städelsches Kunstinstitut und Städtische Galerie Frankfurt am Main, 25. März–20. Juni 1999 (Berlin: Staatliche Museen zu Berlin – Preussischer Kulturbesitz 1998), 108–123.

Ansgar Bach (Hrsg.): *Berlin: Ein literarischer Reiseführer* (Darmstadt: Wissenschaftliche Buchgesellschaft 2007).

Jeremy Barlow: *'The Enraged Musician': Hogarth's Musical Imagery* (Aldershot, Hampshire: Ashgate Publishing Limited 2005).

Gerd Bartoschek: *Die Gemälde im Neuen Palais* (Potsdam-Sanssouci: Generaldirektion der Staatlichen Schlösser und Gärten 1976).

Gerd Bartoschek: *Antoine Pesne, 1683–1757: Ausstellung zum 300. Geburtstag*, Kat. der Ausstellung im Neuen Palais und in den Römischen Bädern Potsdam-Sanssouci, Juni–September 1983, und im Märkischen Museum Berlin, Oktober–Dezember 1983 (Potsdam-Sanssouci: Generaldirektion der Staatlichen Schlösser und Gärten 1983).

Friedrich Benninghoven/Helmut Börsch-Supan/Iselin Grundermann: *Friedrich der Grosse: Ausstellung des Geheimen Staatsarchivs Preußischer Kulturbesitz anläßlich des 200. Todestages König Friedrichs II. von Preußen* (Berlin: Nicolai 1986).

Ekhart Berckenhagen: *Anton Graff: Leben und Werk* (Berlin: Deutscher Verlag für Kunstwissenschaft 1967).

Lance Bertelsen: "The Interior Structures of Hogarth's *Marriage à la Mode*", *Art History* 6, Nr. 2 (1983), 131–142.

David Bindman/Frédéric Ogée/Peter Wagner (Hrsg.): *Hogarth: Representing nature's machines* (Manchester: Manchester University Press 2001).

Thomas Biskup: "Der kinderlose 'roi philosophe'. Herrschertugend und Sexualmoral". In: Bernd Sösemann/Gregor Vogt-Spira (Hrsg.): *Friedrich der Grosse in Europa: Geschichte einer wechselvollen Beziehung*, 2 Bände (Stuttgart: Franz Steiner Verlag 2012), Band I, 21–35.

Tim Blanning: "The representation of Frederick II and George III: a comparison". In: *Öffentliche Tagung des Interdisziplinären Zentrums zur Erforschung der Europäischen Aufklärung an der Martin-Luther-Universität Halle-Wittenberg und der Stiftung Preußische Schlösser und Gärten Ber-*

lin-Brandenburg im Potsdam Museum – Forum für Kunst und Geschichte vom 28.–29. September 2012, hrsg. von Jürgen Luh und Andreas Pečar (Friedrich300 – Colloquien, 8) <http://www.perspectivia.net/content/publikationen/friedrich300-colloquien/friedrich_repraesentation/blanning_representation>

Helmut Börsch-Supan: "Bemerkungen zu einem wiedergefundenen Bildnis Friedrichs des Großen von Georg Wenzeslaus von Knobelsdorff". In: Lucius Grisebach/Konrad Renger (Hrsg.): *Festschrift für Otto von Simson zum 65. Geburtstag* (Frankfurt a. M.: Propyläen Verlag 1977), 398–411.

Helmut Börsch-Supan: "Music in Painting: A Theme in Frederick the Great's Collection", *The Connoisseur* 195 (1977), 31–41.

Helmut Börsch-Supan: *Die Gemälde Antoine Pesnes in den Berliner Schlössern* (Berlin: Verwaltung der Staatlichen Schlösser und Gärten 1982) [*Aus Berliner Schlössern*, 7].

Helmut Börsch-Supan: *Der Maler Antoine Pesne: Franzose und Preusse* (Friedberg: Podzun-Pallas 1986).

Helmut Börsch-Supan: "Friedrich der Große im zeitgenössischen Bildnis". In: Oswald Hauser (Hrsg.): *Friedrich der Große in seiner Zeit* (Köln und Wien. Böhlau Verlag 1987) [*Neue Forschungen zur brandenburg-preußischen Geschichte, Band 8*], 255–270.

Helmut Börsch-Supan: "Friedrichs des Großen Umgang mit Bildern", *Zeitschrift des Deutschen Vereins für Kunstwissenschaft* N.F. 42, Nr. 1 (1988), 23–32.

Wilhelm Bringmann: *Preußen unter Friedrich Wilhelm II. (1786–1797)* (Frankfurt am Main: Peter Lang 2001).

Wilhelm Bringmann: *Friedrich der Große: Ein Porträt* (München: Herbert Utz Verlag 2006).

Klaus Büstrin: "'Ich habe gemeinet, du häst mihr lieb': Friedrichs enge Beziehungen zu seinem Kammerdiener Fredersdorf", *Potsdamer Neueste Nachrichten*, 1. September 2012.

Wolfgang Burgdorf: *Friedrich der Große: Ein biografisches Porträt* (Freiburg im Breisgau: Herder 2011).

Donald Burrows: *Handel*, 2. Aufl. (Oxford und New York: Oxford University Press 2012).

Werner Busch: *Nachahmung als bürgerliches Kunstprinzip. Ikonographische Zitate bei Hogarth und in seiner Nachfolge* (Hildesheim und New York: Georg Olms Verlag 1977).

Werner Busch: *Das sentimentalische Bild: Die Krise der Kunst im 18. Jahrhundert und die Geburt der Moderne* (München: C. H. Beck 1993).

Werner Busch: "Hogarths *Marriage A-la-Mode*: Zur Dialektik von Detailgenauigkeit und Vieldeutigkeit". In: Martina Dillmann/Claude Keisch (Hrsg.): *'Marriage A-la-Mode' – Hogarth und seine deutschen Bewunderer*, Ausst.-Kat., Staatliche Museen zu Berlin, Nationalgalerie – Altes Museum, Berlin, 18. Dezember 1998–28. Februar 1999, Städelsches Kunstinstitut und Städtische Galerie Frankfurt am Main, 25. März–20. Juni 1999 (Berlin: Staatliche Museen zu Berlin – Preussischer Kulturbesitz 1998), 70–83.

Werner Busch: "Die Friedrich-Bilder – der Inbegriff von Menzels Kunst und doch ein gescheitertes Projekt?" In: *Adolph Menzel: Leben und Werk* (München: C. H. Beck 2004), 92–100.

Werner Busch: "Anton Graff und seine Orientierung an der europäischen Porträttradition". In: Marc Fehlmann/Birgit Verwiebe (Hrsg.): *Anton Graff: Gesichter einer Epoche*, Ausst.-Kat., Museum Oskar Reinhart, Winterthur, 22. Juni–29. September 2013; Alte Nationalgalerie, Berlin, 25. Oktober 2013–23. Februar 2014 (München: Hirmer 2013), 168–178.

Edwin von Campe: *Die graphischen Porträts Friedrichs des Großen aus seiner Zeit und ihre Vorbilder* (München: Bruckmann 1958).

Edwin von Campe: *Die graphischen Porträts Friedrichs des Großen aus seiner Zeit und ihre Vorbilder: Ergänzung* (München: Bruckmann 1970).

Giacomo Casanova, Chevalier de Seingalt: *Geschichte meines Lebens*, hrsg. von Erich Loos, übersetzt von Heinz von Sauter, 12 Bände (Berlin: Propyläen Verlag 1964–1967).

Giacomo Casanova, Chevalier de Seingalt: *History of my Life*, Volumes 9 & 10: London, Berlin, Moscow, Petersburg, Warsaw. Translated by Willard R. Trask (Baltimore und London: Johns Hopkins University Press 1997).

Ilias Chrissochoidis: "Handel, Hogarth, Goupy: artistic intersections in early Georgian England", *Early Music* 37, Nr. 4 (2009), 577–596.

Robert L. S. Cowley: *Marriage A-la-Mode: a re-view of Hogarth's narrative art* (Manchester: Manchester University Press 1983).

Louis Crompton: *Homosexuality & Civilization* (Cambridge, MA und London: Belknap Press of Harvard University Press 2003).

Uriel Dann: *Hanover and Great Britain, 1740–1760: Diplomacy and Survival* (Leicester, London: Leicester University Press 1991).

Oliver Das Gupta: "300 Jahre Friedrich der Große – Der schwule Fritz", *Süddeutsche Zeitung*, 23. Januar 2012.

Martin Davies: *National Gallery Catalogues: The British School*, 2. Aufl. (London: National Gallery 1959).

Elisabeth Decultot (Hrsg.): *Briefwechsel von Johann Georg Wille* (Tübingen: Max Niemeyer Verlag 1999).

Paul Dehnert: "Daniel Chodowiecki und der König", *Jahrbuch Preussischer Kulturbesitz* 14 (1977), 307–319.

Paul Dehnert: "Georg Friedrich Schmidt, der Hofkupferstecher des Königs", *Jahrbuch Preussischer Kulturbesitz* 16 (1979), 321–339.

Paul Derks: *Die Schande der heiligen Päderastie: Homosexualität und Öffentlichkeit in der deutschen Literatur 1750 bis 1850* (Berlin: Verlag Rosa Winkel 1990).

Deutsches Historisches Museum (Hrsg.): *Friedrich der Grosse: verehrt, verklärt, verdammt*, Ausst.-Kat., Deutsches Historisches Museum, Berlin, 21. März–26. August 2012 (Stuttgart: Franz Steiner Verlag 2012).

Carl Friedrich-Wilhelm von Diebitsch: *Specielle Zeit- und Geschäfts-Eintheilung König Friedrich des Zweyten* (St. Petersburg: mit Bewilligung der Censur, gedruckt in der Schnoorschen Buchdruckerey 1802).

Martin Disselkamp: *Die Stadt der Gelehrten: Studien zu Johann Joachim Winckelmanns Briefen aus Rom* (Tübingen: Max Niemeyer Verlag 1993).

Hans Dollinger: *Friedrich II. von Preußen: Sein Bild im Wandel von zwei Jahrhunderten* (München: List Verlag 1986).

Carole Dornier: "Orient romanesque et satire de la religion: Claude Crébillon, *Tanzaï et Néadarné* et *Le Sopha*", *Eighteenth-Century Fiction* 11, Nr. 4 (1999), 445–459.

Georges Duplessis (Hrsg.): *Mémoires et journal de J.-G. Wille, graveur du roi: publiés d'après les manuscrits autographes de la Bibliothéque Impériale*, 2 Bände (Paris: Jules Renouard 1857).

John A. Dussinger: "William Hogarth's translation of Watelet on 'Grace' ", *Burlington Magazine* 126 (1984), 691–694.

Robert Eberhardt (Hrsg.): *Anton Graff: Porträts eines Porträtisten* (Berlin: Wolff Verlag 2013).

Judy Egerton: *National Gallery Catalogues: The British School* (London: National Gallery Publications, Distributed by Yale University Press 1998).

Judy Egerton: *Hogarth's 'Marriage A-la-Mode'*, Ausst.-Kat., The National Gallery, London, 15. Oktober 1997–18. Januar 1998.

Judy Egerton: "Zu William Hogarths Zyklus *Marriage A-la-Mode*". In: *'Marriage A-la-Mode' – Hogarth und seine deutschen Bewunderer*, Ausst.-Kat., Staatliche Museen zu Berlin, Nationalgalerie – Altes Museum, Berlin, 18. Dezember 1998–28. Februar 1999, Städelsches Kunstinstitut und Städtische Galerie Frankfurt am Main, 25. März–20. Juni 1999, hrsg. von Martina Dillmann und Claude Keisch (Berlin: Staatliche Museen zu Berlin – Preussischer Kulturbesitz 1998), 22–68.

Elizabeth Einberg: "Milton, St. John and the importance of 'Bottom': Another look at Hogarth's *March of the Guards to Finchley*", *The British Art Journal* 5, Nr. 3 (Winter 2004), 27–34.

Elizabeth Einberg: *The Paintings of William Hogarth: A Catalogue Raisonné* (New Haven und London: Published for the Paul Mellon Centre for Studies in British Art by Yale University Press. In Vorbereitung).

Timothy Erwin: *Textual Vision: Augustan Design and the Invention of Eighteenth-Century British Culture* (Lanham, MD und London: Bucknell University Press; Rowman & Littlefield Publishing Group, Inc. 2015).

Marcin Fabiański: "Correggio's *Jupiter and Io:* Its Sources and Meaning", *Source: Notes in the History of Art* 17, Nr. 1 (1997), 8–14.

Marc Fehlmann/Birgit Verwiebe (Hrsg.): *Anton Graff: Gesichter einer Epoche*, Ausst.-Kat., Museum Oskar Reinhart, Winterthur, 22. Juni–29. September 2013; Alte Nationalgalerie, Berlin, 25. Oktober 2013–23. Februar 2014 (München: Hirmer 2013).

Gerhard Femmel/Christoph Michel: *Die Erotica und Priapea aus den Sammlungen Goethes* (Frankfurt am Main: Insel Verlag 1992).

Dominique Fernandez: *Il ratto di Ganimede: La presenza omosessuale nell'arte e nella società* (Mailand: Bompiani 1991).

Gerd Fesser: "Der König von Rheinsberg: Ein Preuße für heute: Genialisch, kunstsinnig, europäisch und ein bisschen schwul – Prinz Heinrich, Bruder Friedrichs II., wird jetzt in Brandenburg gefeiert", *Die Zeit*, Nr. 32 (1. August 2002).

August Fink: "Herzogin Philippine Charlotte und das Bildnis Friedrichs des Großen", *Braunschweigisches Jahrbuch* 40 (1959), 117–135.

Thomas Fischbacher: *Des Königs Knabe: Friedrich der Große und Antinous* (Weimar: VDG 2011).

Douglas Fordham: "William Hogarth's *The March to Finchley* and the Fate of Comic History Painting", *Art History* 27, Nr. 1 (Februar 2004), 95–128.

Douglas Fordham: *British Art and the Seven Years' War: Allegiance and Autonomy* (Philadelphia: University of Pennsylvania Press, 2010).

Bernadette Fort/Angela Rosenthal (Hrsg.). *The Other Hogarth: Aesthetics of Difference* (Princeton und Oxford: Princeton University Press 2001).

Luba Freedman: "Correggio's *Io* as Reflective of Cinquecento Aesthetic Norms", *Jahrbuch der Kunsthistorischen Sammlungen in Wien* 84 (1988), 93–103.

Katja Frehland-Wildeboer: *Treue Freunde? Das Bündnis in Europa, 1714–1914* (München: Oldenbourg Wissenschaftsverlag 2010).

Ute Frevert: " 'Herr über die Herzen'? Friedrich II. im Zeitalter der Empfindsamkeit". In: Bernd Sösemann/Gregor Vogt-Spira (Hrsg.): *Friedrich der Grosse in Europa: Geschichte einer wechselvollen Beziehung*, 2 Bände (Stuttgart: Franz Steiner Verlag 2012), Band I: 36–51.

Fridericus-Stiche: Eine Hommage an Friedrich den Grossen von Heinrich von Sydow-Zirkwitz für die Friderizianische Gesellschaft zu Berlin (Frankfurt am Main: Edition Sydow 1986).

Friedrich der Große: *Das Palladion: Ein ernsthaftes Gedicht in 6 Gesängen / Le Palladion: Poème grave*, hrsg. von Jürgen Ziechmann, 2 Bände (Bremen: Edition Ziechmann 1985).

Hans-Joachim Giersberg/Claudia Meckel (Hrsg.): *Friedrich II. und die Kunst: Ausstellung zum 200. Todestag*, Ausst. Kat. Neues Palais in Sanssouci Potsdam, 19. Juli–12. Oktober 1986, 2 Bände (Potsdam: Staatliche Schlösser und Gärten 1986).

Tom Goeller: *Der Alte Fritz: Mensch, Monarch, Mythos* (Hamburg: Hoffmann und Campe 2011).

Burkhardt Göres/Claudia Sommer/Detlef Fuchs: *Prinz Heinrich von Preußen: Ein Europäer in Rheinsberg*, Ausst.-Kat., Schloss Rheinsberg, 4. August–27. Oktober 2002, hrsg. von der Stiftung Preußische Schlösser und Gärten Berlin-Brandenburg (München und Berlin: Deutscher Kunstverlag 2002).

70

Johann Wolfgang von Goethe: "Georg Friedrich Schmidt, geboren Berlin 1712, abgegangen daselbst 1775", in: *Goethe's Werke: Vollständige Ausgabe letzter Hand*, Drey und vierzigster Band (Stuttgart und Tübingen: in der J. G. Cotta'schen Buchhandlung 1833), 227–229.

Gisela Groth: "Wie Friedrich II. wirklich aussah", *Preußische Allgemeine Zeitung*, 14. November 2012.

Cecil Gould: *The Paintings of Correggio* (London: Faber and Faber 1976).

Alfred P. Hagemann: "Im Schatten des großen Königs: Königin Elisabeth Christine und ihr Verhältnis zu Friedrich II.". In: *perspectivia.net: Friedrich300 – Friedrich und die historische Größe* <http://www.perspectivia.net/content/publikationen/friedrich300-colloquien/friedrich-groesse/hagemann_schatten>.

Rose-Marie Hagen/Rainer Hagen: "Bühne frei für Lady und Liebhaber: Szenen einer Ehe", *Art: Das Kunstmagazin*, Nr. 10 (Oktober 2001), 78–83.

Mark Hallett: "Foreign Affairs: *Marriage à la Mode*". In: Ders.: *Hogarth* (London: Phaidon Press 2000), 165–196.

James Orchard Halliwell: *A Dictionary of Archaic and Provincial Words, Obsolete Phrases, Proverbs, and Ancient Customs, from the Fourteenth Century*, 2 Bände, 2. Aufl. (London: John Russell Smith 1852).

Johann Georg Hamann: "Des Ritters von Rosencreuz letzte Willensmeinung über den göttlichen und menschlichen Ursprung der Sprache: Aus einer Caricaturbilderurschrift eilfertig übersetzt vom Handlanger des Hierophanten" [1772]. In: Friedrich Roth (Hrsg.): *Hamann's Schriften*, Vierter Theil (Berlin: bey G. Reimer 1823), 21–36.

Handel and the Castrati: The Story Behind the 18th Century Superstar Singers, Aust.-Kat., Handel House Museum, London, 29. März–1. Oktober 2006.

Ellen T. Harris: *Handel as Orpheus: Voice and Desire in the Chamber Cantatas* (Cambridge, MA und London: Harvard University Press 2001).

Ellen T. Harris: "Homosexual Context and Identity: Reflections on the Reception of Handel as Orpheus". In: Chris Mounsey/Caroline Gonda (Hrsg.), *Queer People: Negotiations and Expressions of Homosexuality 1700–1800* (Cranbury, NJ: Associated University Presses 2007), 41–66.

Ellen T. Harris: "Joseph Goupy and George Frideric Handel: From Professional Triumphs to Personal Estrangement", *Huntington Library Quarterly* 71, Nr. 3 (2008), 397–452.

A[rnold] D. Harvey: *Sex in Georgian England: Attitudes and Prejudices from the 1720s to the 1820s* (London: Duckworth & Co. 1994).

Fiona Haslam: *From Hogarth to Rowlandson: Medicine in Art in Eighteenth-Century Britain* (Liverpool: Liverpool University Press 1996).

Sir John Hawkins: *A General History of the Science and Practice of Music*, 5 Bände (London: Printed for T. Payne and Son 1776).

Max Hecker (Hrsg.): *Der Briefwechsel zwischen Goethe und Zelter*, Dritter Band: 1828–1832 (Leipzig: Insel-Verlag 1918).

Werner Hegemann: " 'Die bekannte Schmähliteratur' und die sodomitischen und homosexuellen Anwandlungen Friedrichs II." In: ders.: *Fridericus oder das Königsopfer*. Neue, veränderte, erweiterte Auflage (Hellerau: Jakob Hegner 1926), 698–707.

Eugene E. Helms: *Music at the Court of Frederick the Great* (Norman, OK: University of Oklahoma Press 1960).

Susan W. Henderson: "Frederick the Great of Prussia: A Homophile Perspective", *Gai Saber* 1, Nr. 1 (Spring 1977), 46–54.

Sabine Henze-Döhring: *Friedrich der Große: Musiker und Monarch* (München: C. H. Beck 2012).

Bernd-Ulrich Hergemöller: *Mann für Mann: Biographisches Lexikon* (Frankfurt am Main: Suhrkamp 2001).

Jost Hermand: *Adolph Menzel: Das Flötenkonzert in Sanssouci. Ein realistisch geträumtes Preußenbild* (Frankfurt am Main: Fischer Taschenbuch Verlag 1985).

Philip H. Highfill, Jr./Kalman A. Burnim/Edward A. Langhans: *A Biographical Dictionary of Actors, Actresses, Musicians, Dancers, Managers, and Other Stage Personnel in London, 1660–1800*, Band 15: *Tibbett to M. West* (Carbondale: Southern Illinois University Press 1993).

Arnold Hildebrand: *Das Bildnis Friedrichs des Großen: Zeitgenössische Darstellungen*, 2. Aufl. (Berlin: Nibelungen-Verlag 1942).

Berthold Hinz/Hartmut Krug, et al.: *William Hogarth 1697–1764: Das vollständige graphische Werk*, 2. Aufl. (Gießen: Anabas-Verlag Günter Kämpf KG 1986).

Michael Hirst: "A Drawing of 'The Rape of Ganymede' by Michelangelo". In: Sergio Bertelli/Gloria Ramakus (Hrsg.): *Essays Presented to Myron P. Gilmore* (Florenz: La Nuova Italia Editrice 1978), 253–260.

William Hogarth: *The Analysis of Beauty, with the Rejected Passages from the Manuscript Drafts and Autobiographical Notes*, hrsg. von Joseph Burke (Oxford: Clarendon Press 1955).

William Hogarth: *The Analysis of Beauty*, hrsg. von Ronald Paulson (New Haven und London: Yale University Press 1997).

William Hogarth: *Analyse der Schönheit. Aus dem Englischen von Jörg Heininger. Mit einem Nachwort von Peter Bexte* (Dresden: Verlag der Kunst 1995).

Johann Georg Prinz von Hohenzollern: *Friedrich der Große. Sammler und Mäzen* (München: Hirmer 1992).

Saskia Hüneke: "Friedrich der Grosse in der Bildhauerkunst des 18. und 19. Jahrhunderts", *Jahrbuch/Stiftung Preußische Schlösser und Gärten Berlin-Brandenburg* 2 (1997–1998) [Berlin: Akademie-Verlag 2001], 59–91.

David Hunter: "Mr Handel sings Duets with Lady Gatehouse", *The Handel Institute Newsletter* 17, Nr. 1 (2006), 4–6.

John Ireland: *Hogarth Illustrated*, 2 Bände, 2. Aufl. (London: J. and J. Boydell 1793).

L[udwig] D. Jacoby (Hrsg.): *Schmidt's Werke oder: beschreibendes Verzeichnis sämtlicher Kupferstiche und Radirungen, welche der berühmte Künstler George Friederich Schmidt, Königl. Preuss. Hofkupferstecher, Mitglied der Königl. Academien zu Berlin, Paris und der Kaiserlichen zu St. Petersburg, von Anno 1729 bis zu seinem Tode 1775 verfertigt hat* (Berlin: In Jacoby's Kunsthandlung [...] und in Leipzig bei I. B. G. Fleischer 1815).

Dominic Janes: "Unnatural Appetites: Sodomitical Panic in Hogarth's *The Gate of Calais, or, O the Roast Beef of Old England* (1748)", *Oxford Art Journal* 33, Nr. 1 (2012), 19–31.

Dominic Janes: *Picturing the Closet: Male Secrecy and Homosexual Visibility in Britain* (Oxford und New York: Oxford University Press 2015)

Ursula Pia Jauch: "Eros zwischen Herr und Knecht: Friedrich der Grosse und Francesco Algarotti im Land der Lust". In: Bernd Sösemann (Hrsg.): *Friedrich der Grosse in Europa – gefeiert und umstritten* (Stuttgart: Franz Steiner Verlag 2012), 59–70.

Ursula Pia Jauch: "Annotationen zu den Asylanten, Querdenkern und Avantgardisten in der 'Tafelrunde', oder: Die Gemeinschaft der Epikureer zu Sanssouci". In: Bernd Sösemann/Gregor Vogt-Spira (Hrsg.): *Friedrich der Grosse in Europa: Geschichte einer wechselvollen Beziehung*, 2 Bände (Stuttgart: Franz Steiner Verlag 2012), Band I, 68–111.

Ursula Pia Jauch: *Friedrichs Tafelrunde und Kants Tischgesellschaft: Ein Versuch über Preußen zwischen Eros, Philosophie und Propaganda* (Berlin: Matthes & Seitz 2014).

Hans-Joachim Kadatz/Gerhard Murza: *Georg Wenzeslaus von Knobelsdorff, Baumeister Friedrichs II.* (Leipzig: VEB E. A. Seemann Verlag 1983).

Ernst Hartwig Kantorowicz: *Die zwei Körper des Königs: Eine Studie zur politischen Theologie des Mittelalters. Aus dem Amerikanischen übersetzt von Walter Theimer* (Stuttgart: Klett-Cotta 1992).

72

Claude Keisch: *So malerisch! Menzel und Friedrich der Zweite* (Leipzig: Seemann Henschel 2012).

Gerda Kempter: *Ganymed: Studien zur Typologie* (Köln und Wien: Böhlau 1980).

H[einz] D[ieter] Kittsteiner: *Das Komma von Sans, Souci: Ein Forschungsbericht mit Fußnoten* (Heidelberg: Manutius Verlag 2001).

Anke Klare: "Regent und Reformer: Friedrich II. im Spiegel zeitgenössischer Medaillen", *Jahrbuch Preussischer Kulturbesitz* 48 (2012), 329–361.

Mary Klinger Lindberg: "Dramatic Analogues in William Hogarth's 'Marriage A-la-Mode' ". In: Joachim Möller (Hrsg.): *Hogarth in Context: Ten Essays and a Bibliography* (Marburg: Jonas Verlag 1996), 72–86.

Bernd Kluge: *Die Münzen König Friedrichs II. von Preussen, 1740–1786*. Auf der Grundlage der Werke Friedrich Freiherr von Schrötters neu bearbeitet unter Mitarbeit von Elke Bannicke und Renate Vogel (Berlin: Gebr. Mann 2012) [*Berliner Numismatische Forschungen*, Neue Folge 10].

Andrea M. Kluxen: *Bild eines Königs: Friedrich der Große in der Graphik* (Limburg/Lahn: C. A. Starke 1986).

Kurt Kluxen: *Geschichte Englands: Von den Anfängen bis zur Gegenwart* (Stuttgart: Kröner 1968).

Elfriede R. Knauer: "Zu Correggios Io und Ganymed", *Zeitschrift für Kunstgeschichte* 33 (1970), 61–67.

Ute Christina Koch: " 'Un jour comme l'autre': Ein Tag im Leben Friedrichs in Berichten des 18. und frühen 19. Jahrhunderts". In: *Friederisiko: Friedrich der Große*, Ausst.-Kat., Stiftung Preußische Schlösser und Gärten Berlin-Brandenburg im Neuen Palais und Park Sanssouci, 28. April–28. Oktober 2012, 2 Bände (München: Hirmer 2012), Band I: *Die Ausstellung*, 312–321.

Hubertus Kohle: *Adolph Menzels Friedrich-Bilder: Theorie und Praxis der Geschichtsmalerei im Berlin der 1850er Jahre* (München und Berlin: Deutscher Kunstverlag 2001).

Reinhold Koser (Hrsg.): *Briefwechsel Friedrichs des Großen mit Grumbkow und Maupertuis (1731–1759)* (Leipzig: Verlag von S. Hirzel 1898) [*Publicationen aus den K. Preußischen Staatsarchiven*, 72].

Reinhold Koser: *Geschichte Friedrichs des Großen*, 4 Bände, 4. und 5. vermehrte Auflage (Stuttgart: J. G. Cotta 1912–1913).

Tilman Krause: "Das etwas andere Preußen: Die Historikerin Eva Ziebura über weniger bekannte Züge Friedrichs des Großen, die schwarze Pädagogik des Soldatenkönigs und Homosexualität in Zeiten der Aufklärung", *Welt am Sonntag*, 15. Januar 2012.

Joachim Kruse: *Johann Heinrich Lips, 1758–1817: Ein Zürcher Kupferstecher zwischen Lavater und Goethe* (Coburg: Die Kunstsammlungen der Veste Coburg 1989) [*Kataloge der Kunstsammlungen der Veste Coburg*, Nr. 54].

Anette Kruszynski: *Der Ganymed-Mythos in Emblematik und mythographischer Literatur des 16. Jahrhunderts* (Worms: Wernersche Verlagsgesellschaft 1985).

Bernd W. Krysmanski: *Hogarth's 'Enthusiasm Delineated': Nachahmung als Kritik am Kennertum. Eine Werkanalyse. Zugleich ein Einblick in das sarkastisch-aufgeklärte Denken eines "Künstlerrebellen" im englischen 18. Jahrhundert*, 2 Bände (Hildesheim, Zürich, New York: Georg Olms Verlag 1996).

Bernd Krysmanski: "*O the Roast Beef of Old England*: Hogarth in BSEfreier Zeit vor dem Tor von Calais", *Lichtenberg-Jahrbuch 1997* (Saarbrücken: Saarbrücker Druckerei und Verlag 1998), 29–52.

Bernd Krysmanski: "Lust in Hogarth's *Sleeping Congregation* – Or, How to Waste Time in Post-Puritan England", *Art History* 21, Nr. 3 (September 1998), 393–408.

Bernd W. Krysmanski: *Hogarth's Hidden Parts: Satiric Allusion, Erotic Wit, Blasphemous Bawdiness and Dark Humour in Eighteenth-Century English Art* (Hildesheim, Zürich, New York: Georg Olms Verlag 2010).

B[ernd] Krysmanski: "Hogarth, William". In: *Allgemeines Künstlerlexikon: Die bildenden Künstler aller Zeiten und Völker*, Band 74: Hoelscher-Hornstein, hrsg. von Andreas Beyer, Bénédicte Savoy und Wolf Tegethoff (Berlin und Boston: Walter de Gruyter 2012), 168–176.

Bernd Krysmanski: "Der pädophile Adelsspross: Warum die arrangierte Ehe 'nach der Mode' scheitern musste. Eine Neubewertung von Hogarths *Marriage A-la-Mode* aus sexualgeschichtlicher Sicht zum 250jährigen Todestag des Künstlers", *Lichtenberg-Jahrbuch 2013* (Heidelberg: Universitätsverlag Winter 2015), 57–141.

Bernd W. Krysmanski: "The Paedophilic Husband: Why the Marriage A-la-Mode Failed". In: Bernd W. Krysmanski (Hrsg.): *250 Years On: New Light On William Hogarth: 47 Essays to Commemorate the 250th Anniversary of Hogarth's Death* (Dinslaken: Krysman Press. In Vorbereitung).

Bernd W. Krysmanski: *A Hogarth Bibliography: An Annotated Index on the Source Literature of William Hogarth and his Works. Collated as an Interdisciplinary Research Tool*, 2 Bände (Hildesheim, Zürich, New York: Georg Olms Verlag. In Vorbereitung).

Johannes Kunisch (Hrsg.): *Persönlichkeiten im Umkreis Friedrichs des Großen* (Köln und Wien: Böhlau 1988) [= *Neue Forschungen zur brandenburg-preußischen Geschichte*, Bd. 9].

Johannes Kunisch: *Friedrich der Große: Der König und seine Zeit* (München: C. H. Beck 2004).

Gisold Lammel: *Tagträume: Bilder im Lichte der Aufklärung* (Dresden: Verlag der Kunst 1993).

Johann Caspar Lavater: *Von der Physiognomik: Zweytes Stück, welches einen in allen Absichten sehr unvollkommnen Entwurf zu einem Werke von dieser Art enthält*, Band 2 (Leipzig: bey Weidmanns Erben und Reich 1772).

Johann Caspar Lavater: *Physiognomische Fragmente zur Beförderung von Menschenkenntnis und Menschenliebe*, 4 Bände (Leipzig und Winterthur: Weidmanns Erben und Reich; Heinrich Steiner und Compagnie 1775–1778).

James Lawson: "Hogarth's Plotting of *Marriage à-la-Mode*", *Word & Image* 14, Nr. 3 (Juli–September 1998), 267–80.

Norbert Leithold: *Friedrich der Große: Wie er wirklich war oder: Die beliebtesten Irrtümer über den König von Preußen* (Taucha: Tauchaer Verlag 2005).

Norbert Leithold: *Friedrich der große Hasardeur: Weitere Irrtümer über Friedrich II. von Preußen* (Taucha: Tauchaer Verlag 2006).

Norbert Leithold: *Friedrich II. von Preußen: Ein kulturgeschichtliches Panorama von A–Z* (Berlin: Die Andere Bibliothek 2011).

Norbert Leithold (Hrsg.): *Liebesbriefe und Geheimdepeschen: Aus der Korrespondenz des Grafen Johann Eustach von Goertz mit seiner Gemahlin und Friedrich II. von Preußen 1771 1782* (Berlin: Osburg Verlag 2012).

Norbert Lennartz: "My Unwasht Muse": (De-) Konstruktionen der Erotik in der englischen Literatur des 17. Jahrhunderts (Tübingen: Max Niemeyer Verlag 2009).

Ernst Lewy: "Die Verwandlung Friedrichs des Großen: Eine psychoanalytische Untersuchung", *Psyche* 49 (1995), 726–804.

Georg Christoph Lichtenberg: *Schriften und Briefe*, Band III: *Aufsätze, Entwürfe, Gedichte, Erklärung der Hogarthischen Kupferstiche*, hrsg. von Wolfgang Promies (München: Carl Hanser Verlag 1972).

Viktor Link: "The Reception of Crébillon's *Le Sopha* in England: An Unnoticed Edition and Some Imitations", *Studies on Voltaire and the Eighteenth Century* 132 (1975), 199–203.

Leonardo de Lorenzo: *My Complete Story of the Flute: The Instrument, the Performer, the Music* (Lubbock: Texas Tech University Press 1992).

N. F. Lowe: "Hogarth, Beauty Spots, and sexually transmitted Diseases", *British Journal for Eighteenth Century Studies* 15, Nr. 1 (Spring 1992), 71–79.

N. F. Lowe: "The Meaning of Venereal Disease in Hogarth's Graphic Art". In: Linda E. Merians (Hrsg.): *The Secret Malady: Venereal Disease in Eighteenth-Century Britain and France* (Lexington: University Press of Kentucky 1996), 168–182.

Jürgen Luh: *Der Große: Friedrich II. von Preußen* (München: Siedler 2011).

Jürgen Luh: "Freundschaften? – Verhältnisse. Friedrich und seine Vertrauten". In: *Friederisiko: Friedrich der Große*, Ausst.-Kat., Stiftung Preußische Schlösser und Gärten Berlin-Brandenburg im Neuen Palais und Park Sanssouci, 28. April–28. Oktober 2012, 2 Bände (München: Hirmer 2012), Band I: *Die Ausstellung*, 330–341.

Jean Lulvès: *Das einzige glaubwürdige Bildnis Friedrichs des Großen als König* (Hannover und Leipzig: Hahn 1913).

Thomas McGeary: "Handel and Homosexuality: Burlington House and Cannons Revisited", *Journal of the Royal Musical Association* 136, Nr. 1 (Mai 2011), 33–71.

Frauke Mankartz: "Die Marke Friedrich: Der preußische König im zeitgenössischen Bild". In: *Friederisiko: Friedrich der Große*, Ausst.-Kat., Stiftung Preußische Schlösser und Gärten Berlin-Brandenburg im Neuen Palais und Park Sanssouci, 28. April–28. Oktober 2012, 2 Bände (München: Hirmer 2012), Band I: *Die Ausstellung*, 204–221.

Marcella Marongiu: "Il fanciullo amato da Giove: Il Ganimede di Michelangelo a Firenze", *Art e Dossier* 17, Nr. 180 (2002), 27–32.

Stefania Massari: *Giulio Romano pinxit et delineavit: Opere grafiche autografe di collaborazione e bottega*, Ausst.-Kat., Palazzo della Farnesina, Rom, 11. Februar–10. April 1993 (Rom: Fratelli Palombi 1993).

Sarah Maza/Sean Shesgreen: "Marriage in the French and English Manners: Hogarth and Abraham Bosse", in Bernadette Fort/Angela Rosenthal (Hrsg.): *The Other Hogarth: Aesthetics of Difference* (Princeton: Princeton University Press 2001), 192–211.

"Memoirs of Mr. William Hogarth", *Annual Register* 7 (Dezember 1764), 62–64.

Karl Adolf Menzel: *Neuere Geschichte der Deutschen von der Reformation bis zur Bundes-Acte*, Zehnter Band: *Die Zeit Karls VI. und die Anfänge Friedrichs II.* (Breslau: Druck und Verlag von Graß, Barth und Comp. 1843).

Detlef Merten: *Der Katte-Prozeß: Vortrag gehalten vor der Berliner Juristischen Gesellschaft am 14. Februar 1979* (Berlin: Walter de Gruyter 1980) [*Schriftenreihe der Juristischen Gesellschaft zu Berlin*, 62].

Richard Meyer: "Nature Revers'd: Satire and Homosexual Difference in Hogarth's London". In: Bernadette Fort/Angela Rosenthal (Hrsg.): *The Other Hogarth: Aesthetics of Difference* (Princeton: Princeton University Press 2001), 162–173.

Rainer Michaelis: "Kronprinz Friedrich von Preußen en miniature: Notizen zu einer Arbeit Antoine Pesnes", *Pantheon* 54 (1996), 190–192.

Rainer Michaelis: "Betrachtungen zum malerischen Werk des preussischen Hofkupferstechers Georg Friedrich Schmidt (1712–1775)", *Jahrbuch Preussischer Kulturbesitz* 35 (1998) [1999], 221–235.

Rainer Michaelis: *Antoine Pesne (1683–1757): Die Werke des preußischen Hofmalers in der Berliner Gemäldegalerie* (Berlin: Gemäldegalerie Staatliche Museen zu Berlin 2003).

Rainer Michaelis: "Friedrich der Große im Spiegel der Werke des Daniel Nikolaus Chodowiecki". In: *Friederisiko: Friedrich der Große*, Ausst.-Kat., Stiftung Preußische Schlösser und Gärten Berlin-Brandenburg im Neuen Palais und Park Sanssouci, 28. April–28. Oktober 2012, 2 Bände (München: Hirmer 2012), Band II: *Die Essays*, 262–271.

Robert Mode: "Still 'Marching to Finchley': Hogarth, Coram, and the Two Fredericks", in Bernd W. Krysmanski (Hrsg.): *250 Years On: New Light On William Hogarth: 47 Essays to Commemorate the 250th Anniversary of Hogarth's Death* (Dinslaken: Krysman Press. In Vorbereitung).

Carol Morganti: "Il mito di Ganimede nei disegni e nelle incisioni del Rinascimento", *Grafica d'arte* 16, Nr. 62 (2005), 4–15.

Wolfgang Müller: "Seid reinlich bei Tage und säuisch bei Nacht (Goethe) oder: Betrachtungen über die schönste Sache der Welt im Spiegel der deutschen Sprache – einst und jetzt?". In: Rudolf Hoberg (Hrsg.): *Sprache – Erotik – Sexualität* (Berlin: Erich Schmidt Verlag 2001), 11–61.

Hans-Joachim Neumann: *Friedrich der Große: Feldherr und Philosoph* (Berlin: Ed. q. 2000).

Friedrich Nicolai (Hrsg.): *Anekdoten von König Friedrich II. von Preussen, und von einigen Personen, die um Ihn waren*, Sechs Hefte (Berlin und Stettin 1788–1792).

Friedrich Nicolai: *Anekdoten von Friedrich dem Großen und von einigen Personen, die um ihn waren* (Ausgewählte Neuauflage, München o.J.).

John Nichols et al.: *Biographical Anecdotes of William Hogarth: With a Catalogue of his Works chronologically arranged, and occasional Remarks*, 2. Aufl. (London: Printed by and for J. Nichols 1782).

John Nichols/George Steevens: *The Genuine Works of William Hogarth, illustrated with Biographical Anecdotes, a Chronological Catalogue and Commentary*, 2 Bände (London: Printed for Longman, Hurst, Rees, and Orme 1808–1810).

Felicity A. Nussbaum: "Between 'Oriental' and 'Blacks So Called', 1688–1788". In: Daniel Carey/ Lynn Festa (Hrsg.): *The Postcolonial Enlightenment: Eighteenth-Century Colonialism and Postcolonial Theory* (Oxford und New York: Oxford University Press 2009), 137–166.

Martina Ochs: "Sexualität in *Le Sopha* von Crébillon Fils". Studienarbeit, Universität des Saarlandes (München: GRIN 1995).

Wolfgang von Oettingen: "Daniel Chodowieckis Arbeiten für Friedrich den Großen und seine Darstellungen der königlichen Familie", *Hohenzollern-Jahrbuch* 8 (1904), 1–18.

Œuvres posthumes de Frédéric II, Roi de Prusse, Tome VIII: *Poésies* – Tome II (Amsterdam 1789).

Frédéric Ogée: "L'œil erre: les parcours sériels de Hogarth", *l'Errance, Tropismes* [Université de Paris X – Nanterre], 5 (1991), 39–105.

Frédéric Ogée (Hrsg.): *The Dumb show: Image and society in the works of William Hogarth* (Oxford: Voltaire Foundation 1997) [*Studies on Voltaire and the Eighteenth Century*, 357].

Frédéric Ogée: "William Hogarth and Otherness: The Case of France". In Anja Müller/Achim Hescher/Anke Uebel (Hrsg.): *Representing Restoration, Enlightenment and Romanticism: Studies in New-Eighteenth-Century Literature and Film in Honour of Hans-Peter Wagner* (Trier: WVT Wissenschaftlicher Verlag Trier 2014), xxvii–xxxvii.

Stephen Orgel: "Ganymede Agonistes", *GLQ: A Journal of Lesbian and Gay Studies* 10, Nr. 3 (2004), 485–501.

Erwin Panofsky: "Die neuplatonische Bewegung und Michelangelo". In: ders.: *Studien zur Ikonologie: Humanistische Themen in der Kunst der Renaissance* (Köln: DuMont Buchverlag 1980), 251–326.

J. D. Passavant: *Rafael von Urbino und sein Vater Giovanni Santi*, Zweiter Theil (Leipzig: F. A. Brockhaus 1839).

Ronald Paulson: *Hogarth: His Life, Art, and Times*, 2 Bände (New Haven und London: Yale University Press 1971).

Ronald Paulson: *The Art of Hogarth* (London: Phaidon Press 1975).

Ronald Paulson: *Hogarth's Graphic Works*, Third, Revised Edition (London: The Print Room 1989).

Ronald Paulson: *Hogarth, Volume 2: High Art and Low, 1732–1750* (Cambridge: Lutterworth Press 1992).

Ronald Paulson: *Hogarth, Volume 3: Art and Politics, 1750–1764* (Cambridge: Lutterworth Press 1993).

Ronald Paulson: *Hogarth's Harlot: Sacred Parody in Enlightenment England* (Baltimore und London: Johns Hopkins University Press 2003).

Ulrich Pfisterer: "Zwei Körper des Königs". In: Uwe Fleckner/Martin Warnke/Hendrik Ziegler (Hrsg.): *Politische Ikonographie: Ein Handbuch*, 2 Bände (München: C. H. Beck 2011), Band II: Imperator bis Zwerg, 557–564.

Martin Postle: "Hogarth's *Marriage A-la-Mode*, scene III: A re-inspection of 'The Inspection' ", *Apollo* 146 (November 1997), 38–39.

Bernhard von Poten: "Keith, Peter Karl Christof". In: *Allgemeine Deutsche Biographie*, Band 15 (Leipzig: Duncker & Humblot 1882), 555.

Numa Praetorius [= Eugen Wilhelm]: "Die Homosexualitat des Prinzen Heinrich von Preußen, des Bruders Friedrichs des Großen", *Zeitschrift für Sexualwissenschaft* 15 (1929), 465–476.

Bruno Preisendörfer: "Das Bildnis des Königs". In: ders.: *Staatsbildung als Königskunst: Ästhetik und Herrschaft im preußischen Absolutismus* (Berlin: Akademie Verlag 2000), 83–110.

J[ohann] D. E. Preuß: *Friedrich der Große: Eine Lebensgeschichte*, 5 Bände (Berlin: In der Nauckschen Buchhandlung 1832–1834).

Fritz J. Raddatz: "Weiberfeind und Kirchenhasser: Friedrich II. als Schriftsteller". In: Ders.: *Das Rot der Freiheitssonne wurde Blut: Literarische Essays* (Springe: zu Klampen Verlag 2007), 66–77.

Elke von Radziewsky: "Menzel – ein Realist?" In: Werner Hofmann (Hrsg.): *Menzel – der Beobachter* (München: Prestel 1982), 17–30.

K. F. Reiche: *Friedrich der Große und seine Zeit: Nach den besten Quellen dargestellt* (Leipzig: Christian Ernst Kollmann 1840).

Alan Riding: "In Opera, a Different Kind of Less Is More: 'Handel and the Castrati' ", *New York Times*, 19. April 2006.

Christine Riding: "Marriage A-la-Mode". In: Mark Hallett/Christine Riding: *Hogarth*, Ausst.-Kat. Musée du Louvre, Paris, 18. Oktober 2006–7. Januar 2007; Tate Britain, London, 7. Februar–29. April 2007; CaixaForum, Barcelona, 29. Mai–26. August 2007 (London: Tate Publishing 2006), 140–157.

Karl Heinrich Siegfried Rödenbeck: *Tagebuch oder Geschichtskalender aus Friedrich's des Großen Regentenleben (1740–1786)*, Band 1 (Berlin: Verlag der Plahn'schen Buchhandlung 1840).

James M. Saslow: *Ganymede in the Renaissance: Homosexuality in Art and Society* (New Haven und London: Yale University Press 1986).

Nina Simone Schepkowski: *Johann Ernst Gotzkowsky: Kunstagent und Gemäldesammler im friderizianischen Berlin* (Berlin: Akademie Verlag 2009).

Martin Schieder: "Die auratische Abwesenheit des Königs: Zum schwierigen Umgang Friedrichs des Großen mit dem eigenen Bildnis". In: Bernd Sösemann/Gregor Vogt-Spira (Hrsg.): *Friedrich der Große in Europa: Geschichte einer wechselvollen Beziehung*, 2 Bände (Stuttgart: Franz Steiner Verlag 2012), Band I, 325–338.

Norbert Schmitz: *Der italienische Freund: Francesco Algarotti und Friedrich der Große* (Hannover: Wehrhahn Verlag 2012).

Rainer Schoch: *Das Herrscherbild in der Malerei des 19. Jahrhunderts* (München: Prestel Verlag 1975).

Karin Schrader: *Der Bildnismaler Johann Georg Ziesenis (1717–1776): Leben und Werk mit kritischem Oeuvrekatalog* (Münster: LIT Verlag 1995).

Hans Schumacher (Hrsg.): *Francesco Algarotti: Ein philosophischer Hofmann im Jahrhundert der Aufklärung* (Hannover: Wehrhahn Verlag 2009).

Paul Seidel: "Friedrich der Große als Sammler von Gemälden und Skulpturen", *Jahrbuch der Königlich Preußischen Kunstsammlungen* 13 (1892), 183–212.

Paul Seidel: "Friedrich der Große als Sammler. Fortsetzung und Nachtrag", *Jahrbuch der Königlich Preußischen Kunstsammlungen* 15 (1894), 48–57, 81–93.

Paul Seidel: "Georg Friedrich Schmidt, der erste Illustrator und Drucker Friedrichs des Großen", *Hohenzollern-Jahrbuch* 5 (1901), 60–73.

Paul Seidel: *Friedrich der Grosse und die bildende Kunst* (Leipzig und Berlin: Giesecke & Devrient 1922).

Hans-Ulrich Seifert: "Editorische Miszellen zur Entdeckung der 'Lust': Ein Gedicht kommt wieder ans Licht". In: Bernd Sösemann (Hrsg.): *Friedrich der Grosse in Europa – gefeiert und umstritten* (Stuttgart: Franz Steiner Verlag 2012), 71–76.

Desmond Shawe-Taylor (Hrsg.): *The first Georgians: Art & Monarchy 1714–1760* (London: Royal Collection Trust 2014).

Sean Shesgreen (Hrsg.): *Engravings by Hogarth: 101 Prints* (New York: Dover Publications, Inc. 1973).

Robin Simon: "Un rosbif à Paris: Hogarth's visit to Paris in 1743", *The British Art Journal* 7, Nr. 2 (Autumn 2006), 24–33.

Robin Simon: *Hogarth, France and British Art: The rise of the arts in eighteenth-century Britain* (London: Hogarth Arts, Distributed by Paul Holberton Publishing 2007).

William C. Smith: "Handel's Failure in 1745: New Letters", in: *Concerning Handel: His Life and Works. Essays by William C. Smith* (London: Cassell & Co. 1948), 145–161.

Louis L[eo] Snyder (Hrsg.): *Frederick the Great* (Englewood Cliffs: Prentice-Hall 1971).

Hans-Bernd Spies/Helmut Winter (Hrsg.): *Die Schlacht bei Dettingen 1743: Beiträge zum 250. Jahrestag* (Aschaffenburg: Geschichts- und Kunstverein Aschaffenburg e. V. 1993) [*Veröffentlichungen des Geschichts- und Kunstvereins Aschaffenburg e. V.*, Band 38].

William Barclay Squire: "Handel in 1745". In: Carl Mennicke (Hrsg.): *Riemann-Festschrift: Gesammelte Studien, Hugo Riemann zum sechzigsten Geburtstage überreicht von Freunden und Schülern* (Leipzig: Max Hesse 1909), 423–433.

James D. Steakley: "Sodomy in Enlightenment Prussia", *Journal of Homosexuality* 16, Nr. 1–2 (1988), 163–175.

Frederic George Stephens/Edward Hawkins: *Catalogue of Prints and Drawings in the British Museum*, Division I: *Political and Personal Satires*, Band III, Teil I (London: British Museum, Printed by Order of the Trustees 1877).

Karl M. Swoboda: "Die Io und der Ganymed des Correggio in der Wiener Gemäldegalerie". In: ders.: *Kunst und Geschichte: Vorträge und Aufsätze* (Wien, Köln und Graz: Hermann Böhlaus Nachf. 1969), 165–179.

Günther Thiersch: "Das Flötenkonzert". In: ders.: *Deutsche Maler im 19. Jahrhundert: Zwanzig Meisterwerke aus dem Besitz der Nationalgalerie Berlin, Staatliche Museen Preußischer Kulturbesitz* (Stuttgart: Ernst Klett Verlag 1979), 130–140.

Gary C. Thomas: " 'Was George Frideric Handel Gay?' On Closet Questions and Cultural Politics". In: Philip Brett/Elizabeth Wood/Gary C. Thomas (Hrsg.): *Queering the Pitch: The New Gay and Lesbian Musicology*, 2. Aufl. (New York und Abingdon: Routledge 2006), 155–203.

Andrew C. Thompson: *George II: King and Elector* (New Haven und London: Yale University Press 2011).

Jenny Uglow: *Hogarth: A Life and a World* (London: Faber and Faber 1997).

Veit Veltzke (Hrsg.): *Macht und Dienst: Zur Darstellung des brandenburgisch-preußischen Herrscherhauses in Gemälde und Graphik 1650–1900, Ausst.-Kat.*, Städtische Galerie im Centrum Wesel, 17. Oktober–7. November 1993; Schloss Cappenberg, 25. November 1993–27. Februar 1994 (Minden und Wesel. Preußen-Museum Nordrhein-Westfalen 1993).

Voltaire: *Über den König von Preußen: Memoiren*, hrsg. und übersetzt von Anneliese Botond (Frankfurt am Main: Insel Verlag 1967) [Insel-Bücherei, 892].

Voltaire: *Memoirs of the Life of Monsieur de Voltaire written by himself*, translated by Andrew Brown (London: Hesperus 2007).

Gustaf Berthold Volz: "Friedrich der Große und seine sittlichen Ankläger", *Forschungen zur Brandenburgischen und Preußischen Geschichte* 41 (1928), 1–37.

Peter Jan de Voogd, et al.: "A Reading of William Hogarth's *Marriage à la Mode*". In: Jacques B. H. Alblas/Richard Todd (Hrsg.): *From Caxton to Beckett: Essays presented to W. H. Toppen on the occasion of his seventieth birthday* (Amsterdam: Rodopi 1979), 69–99.

Peter Jan de Voogd: "Generation in William Hogarth's *Marriage à-la-Mode*". In: Serge Soupel (Hrsg.): *Les âges de la vie en Grande-Bretagne au XVIIIe siècle: Actes du colloque décembre 1990 et décembre 1991* (Paris: Centre d'Etudes Anglaises du XVIIIe siècle de l'Université de la Sorbonne Nouvelle Paris III 1995), 47–55.

Gaston Vorberg: *Der Klatsch über das Geschlechtsleben Friedrichs II. – Der Fall Jean-Jacques Rousseau* (Bonn: A. Marcus und E. Webers Verlag 1921) [*Abhandlungen aus dem Gebiete der Sexualforschung*, Band 3, Heft 6].

Peter Wagner: *Eros Revived: Erotica of the Enlightenment in England and America* (London: Secker & Warburg 1988).

Hans-Peter Wagner: "Eroticism in Graphic Art: The Case of William Hogarth". In: Patricia B. Craddock/Carla H. Hay (Hrsg.): *Studies in Eighteenth-Century Culture* 21 (1991), 53–74.

Peter Wagner: "Eighteenth-Century Sexual 'Mentalités' in William Hogarth's Graphic Art". In: Jürgen Klein (Hrsg.): *State, Science and Modernization in England from the Renaissance to the Modern Times: Herborn Symposion 1990* (Hildesheim, Zürich, New York: Georg Olms Verlag 1994), 190–221.

Peter Wagner: "Spotting the Symptoms: Hogarthian Bodies as Sites of Semantic Ambiguity". In: Bernadette Fort/Angela Rosenthal (Hrsg.): *The Other Hogarth: Aesthetics of Difference* (Princeton: Princeton University Press 2001), 102–119.

Peter Wagner: "The Artistic Framing of English Nationalism in Hogarth's *The Gate of Calais, or, The Roast Beef of Old England*". In: Frédéric Ogée (Hrsg.): *'Better In France?' The Circulation of Ideas Across the Channel in the Eighteenth Century* (Lewisburg, PA: Bucknell University Press, 2005), 71–87.

Peter Wagner: "Minding the Gaps: Ellipses in William Hogarth's Narrative Art". In: Peter Wagner/ Frédéric Ogée/Robert Mankin/Achim Hescher (Hrsg.): *The Ruin and the Sketch in the Eighteenth Century* (Trier: Wissenschaftlicher Verlag Trier 2008), 121–152.

Peter Wagner: "Anti-Taste: Hogarth and the Obscene". In: Peter Wagner/Frédéric Ogée (Hrsg.), *Taste and the Senses in the Eighteenth Century* (Trier: WVT Wissenschaftlicher Verlag Trier 2011) [*Landau Paris Studies on the Eighteenth Century*, 3], 381–396.

Hans-Peter Wagner: *William Hogarth: Das graphische Werk: Ein kommentierter Auswahlkatalog* (Trier: WVT Wissenschaftlicher Verlag Trier 2013).

Robert R. Wark: "Hogarth's Narrative Method in Practice and Theory". In: H[ugh] T[homas] Swedenberg (Hrsg.): *England in the Restoration and Early Eighteenth Century: Essays on Culture and Society* (Berkeley, Los Angeles, London: University of California Press 1972), 161–172.

Reinhard Wegner: "Friedrich der Große und die englische Kunst", *Zeitschrift des Deutschen Vereins für Kunstwissenschaft* N.F. 42, Nr. 1 (1988), 49–59.

Brunhilde Wehinger (Hrsg.): *Geist und Macht: Friedrich der Große im Kontext der europäischen Kulturgeschichte* (Berlin: Akademie Verlag 2005).

Ute-G. Weickardt/Tigo Eggeling (Hrsg.): *„Zum Maler und zum Großen Architekten geboren": Georg Wenzeslaus von Knobelsdorff. 1699–1753*, Katalog zur Ausstellung zum 300. Geburtstag, Weißer Saal im Schloß Charlottenburg, 18. Februar–25 April 1999 (Berlin: Generaldirektion der Stiftung Preußische Schlösser und Gärten Berlin-Brandenburg 1999).

Arthur S. Wensinger/William B. Coley (Hrsg.): *Hogarth on High Life: The 'Marriage à la Mode' Series from Georg Christoph Lichtenberg's Commentaries* (Middletown, CT: Wesleyan University Press 1970).

J[oseph] E[duard] Wessely: *Georg Friedrich Schmidt: Verzeichniss seiner Stiche und Radirungen* (Hamburg: Haendcke & Lehmkuhl 1887).

Geraldine D. Wind: " 'Sport for Jove': Correggio's 'Io' and 'Ganymede' ", *Gazette des Beaux-Arts*, 6. Pér. 109, Nr. 1418 (1987), 106–108.

Franziska Windt: "Künstlerische Inszenierung von Größe: Friedrichs Selbstdarstellung im Neuen Palais". In: *Friederisiko: Friedrich der Große*, Ausst.-Kat., Stiftung Preußische Schlösser und Gärten Berlin-Brandenburg im Neuen Palais und Park Sanssouci, 28. April–28. Oktober 2012, 2 Bände (München: Hirmer 2012), Band II: *Die Essays*, 130–149.

Werner Wolf: "Das Problem der Narrativität in Literatur, bildender Kunst und Musik: Ein Beitrag zu einer intermedialen Erzähltheorie". In: Vera Nünning/Ansgar Nünning (Hrsg.): *Erzähltheorie transgenerisch, intermedial, interdisziplinär* (Trier: Wissenschaftlicher Verlag Trier 2002) [*WVT-Handbücher zum literaturwissenschaftlichen Studium*, 5], 23–104.

Joseph Wright (Hrsg.): *The English Dialect Dictionary, Being the Complete Vocabulary of all Dialect Words Still in Use, or Known to have been in Use during the Last Two Hundred Years*, 6 Bände (London: Henry Frowde 1898–1905).

David Wykes: "Hogarth and Rigaud: One Portrait", *Notes and Queries* 36, Nr. 4 (Dezember 1989), 470–475.

Eva Ziebura: *Prinz Heinrich von Preußen* (Berlin: Stapp Verlag 1999).

Jürgen Ziechmann: *Fridericianische Encyclopédie: Friedrich der Große und seine Epoche – Das Lexikon – Ereignisse, Personen, Sachverhalte* (Bremen: Verlagskooperative H. M. Hauschild und Edition Ziechmann 2011).

[Johann Georg] Ritter von Zimmermann: *Fragmente über Friedrich den Grossen zur Geschichte seines Lebens, seiner Regierung, und seines Charakters*, 3 Bände (Leipzig: in der Weidmannischen Buchhandlung 1790).

"Zu den Vignetten: Der Berliner Hofkupferstecher Georg Friedrich Schmidt (1712–1775)". In: Jürgen Overhoff/Vanessa de Senarclens (Hrsg.): *Friedrich der Große: An meinen Geist: Friedrich der Große in seiner Dichtung. Eine Anthologie* (Paderborn: Ferdinand Schöningh 2011), 309–312.

Stichwortverzeichnis

English Index

Über den Autor

Bernd Krysmanski studierte Biologie an der Universität Düsseldorf, Freie Graphik und Kunsterziehung an der Kunstakademie Düsseldorf und Kunstgeschichte an der Ruhr-Universität Bochum. Er promovierte bei Werner Busch mit einer zweibändigen Studie über den englischen Maler und Graphiker William Hogarth, schrieb wissenschaftliche Aufsätze für eine Reihe renommierter Fachzeitschriften – wie *The Art Bulletin—Art History—The British Journal for Eighteenth-Century Studies—1650–1850: Ideas, Aesthetics, and Inquiries in the Early Modern Era—Studies on Voltaire and the Eighteenth Century* oder das *Lichtenberg-Jahrbuch* – und ist Autor und Herausgeber mehrerer Bücher über Hogarth. Zu letzteren zählt der bei Georg Olms erschienene Band *Hogarth's Hidden Parts: Satiric Allusion, Erotic Wit, Blasphemous Bawdiness and Dark Humour in Eighteenth-Century English Art* (2010), in dem alle zweideutig-sexuell getönten Motive in Hogarths Oeuvre näher analysiert werden. Krysmanski verfasste auch den Übersichtsartikel über Hogarth in Band 74 des *Allgemeinen Künstlerlexikons: Die bildenden Künstler aller Zeiten und Völker* (2012) und ist seit rund zwei Jahrzehnten dabei, eine zweibändige, internationale Hogarth-Bibliographie zusammenzustellen, die kurz vor dem Abschluss steht. Ebenfalls bei Krysman Press erscheint – etwas verspätet – unter dem Titel *250 Years On: New Light On William Hogarth: 47 Essays to Commemorate the 250th Anniversary of Hogarth's Death* der umfangreiche, vom Autor edierte Sammelband zum 250jährigen Todestag von William Hogarth, an dem 38 Experten aus 9 Ländern mitgewirkt haben.

Acknowledgments

The author would like to thank Brian Nattress for his support in translating the main text of this study into appropriate English, especially as this work was done at short notice. The idea to provide the international reader with more than a mere summary in English arose only a few weeks before publication. My thanks also to Charles Harrison-Wallace for his additional last-minute suggestions.

By the same author

HOGARTH'S HIDDEN PARTS
Bernd W. Krysmanski

OLMS

Bernd W. Krysmanski

Hogarth's Hidden Parts

Satiric Allusion, Erotic Wit, Blasphemous Bawdiness and Dark Humour in Eighteenth-Century English Art

Hildesheim · Zurich · New York: Georg Olms Verlag 2010

514 pages, 304 illustrations

ISBN 978-3-487-14471-9

€ 48.00

If you think of William Hogarth chiefly as a social moralist who provided ethical guidance through his pictorial satires and gave charitable support to foundlings, then it is high time you changed your mind. This challenging, thoroughly researched and thought-provoking book reveals many new findings on Hogarth, showing us a different, hidden and immoral English artist: a carouser, a debauchee, and a spiteful joker who mercilessly attacked his contemporaries. Although on the surface an honest pictorial satirist and a successful print-dealer, Hogarth nevertheless wallowed in obscene amusement, frequented prostitutes, was possibly interested in the sexuality of children, and seemingly died from the lingering effects of syphilis. Hogarth the popular painter and engraver is presented here as a dark humorist who dealt primarily in sexual *double entendre* and produced, within his witty and extremely profane genre scenes, blasphemous motifs that satirically lambasted "high" religious art and debunked the eighteenth-century taste for Italianate Old Master work. As this book contains, in addition, many new and surprising findings on numerous canonical works—among them *The Four Stages of Cruelty; Industry and Idleness; Sigismunda; Boys Peeping at Nature; Before* and *After;* Plate 2 of *The Analysis of Beauty; Noon* and *Evening; Marriage A-la-Mode; A Rake's Progress; Chairing the Members; Paul before Felix* and its burlesqued version; *David Garrick and his Wife; Transubstantiation Satirized;* and *Enthusiasm Delineated*—it ought to change the way we think about Hogarth the pictorial satirist.

From reviews of the book

The tone is brisk and the author covers a large amount of material with efficacy. [...] Krysmanski's claim is that Hogarth included shocking, irreverent, and sexually allusive motifs in publicly circulated images. The reasons for this would be threefold: first, because he was playing to contemporary taste; second, because the visual interest of an allusion is amplified when it is stumbled upon by the viewer. The third reason would be provocation, in that the motifs were placed as subtle bait to irritate the artist's enemies, and notably the connoisseurs of the polite. [...] Scholars with an interest in the "everything and anything" of Hogarthian scholarship may well find the publication useful.

Kate Grandjouan, Eighteenth-Century Studies 45, no. 2 (Winter 2012), 335–336.

[...] even today works of scholarship flaunting the words "desire" or "erotic" in their titles, will, when written by Americans, have very little in them of the venereal or libidinous. In *Hogarth's Hidden Parts*, there is a great deal which is new, valuable, and erotic. [...] *Hogarth's Hidden Parts* is a volume of immense scholarship, based on exhaustive and thoughtful readings in the literature of art and social history (...). It cites a mountain of books and articles on Hogarth, some of which were new to me as a Hogarth scholar. Predictably but happily, *Hogarth's Hidden Parts* references and documents many neglected works in German on English art as well as general works that bear on the engraver and his age. It is also a study of great breadth, both in the works Mr. Krysmanski analyzes and in the themes he treats, making it a small encyclopedia on Hogarth (as well as on his aesthetic and literary relationships). It is particularly strong in locating Hogarth in the context of European art, an undertaking begun by Frederic Antal and extended further here. In this respect, the illustrations to Mr. Krysmanski's book are generous and helpful; in all, the volume offers 304 images, some of them arcane and difficult to find. The book is carefully and exhaustively indexed, devoting fifty pages to citing themes, artists, museums, collections, and historical figures; it is notably generous in how it cites and credits modern scholars. In all these respects, *Hogarth's Hidden Parts* stands as a lively, iconoclastic commentary that must be consulted and reckoned with by any serious art historian.

Sean Shesgreen, The Scriblerian 45, no. 2 (2013), 260–262.

Krysmanski's wonderfully teeming, keen-sighted rogues' gallery will no doubt facilitate new and complex understandings of Hogarth's oeuvre. In particular, the book provides a treasure trove of raw material for scholars interested in the changing perceptions of sex, gender, and the body; the impact of urbanization, commodification, and secularization; and the intersection of high and low culture in the eighteenth century. At its best, Krysmanski's book provides a marvelously thorough registry (the book contains over three hundred illustrations) of the many instances of erotic, scatological, sadistic, irreligious, and otherwise subversive motifs in Hogarth's art. [...] Krysmanski's project of aggregating his motifs systematically, and of displaying them alongside other examples of the same motif (taken both from within and from outside Hogarth's own body of work)—in addition to his discovery (promised in the title) of hitherto unnoticed details—can result, at many points, in real revelations.

Katherine Mannheimer, *The Eighteenth Century* 54, no. 4 (Winter 2013), 559–564.

Die vielen Abbildungen und ihre höchst instruktive Erläuterung, die materialreichen Fußnoten, schließlich auch die umfangreiche Bibliographie sowie ein sorgfältig erstellter Index machen das angenehm lesbare und in der Hand liegende Buch zu einer Fundgrube für jeden, der mehr über die frivolen, obszönen und blasphemischen Aspekte der Kunst des 18. Jahrhunderts wissen möchte.

Till Kinzel, *Germanisch-Romanische Monatsschrift*, N.F. 64, Nr. 1 (2014), 104–105.

Forthcoming Publication

250 Years On
New Light On William Hogarth

47 Essays to Commemorate the 250th Anniversary of Hogarth's Death

Edited by Bernd W. Krysmanski

Incorporating contributions by distinguished authors and an up-and-coming generation of younger art and literary historians, this 1000-page volume of essays on William Hogarth and his work offers unparalleled abundance and variety. Thirty-eight scholars from Australia, Canada, France, Germany, Italy, the Netherlands, New Zealand, the UK and USA have agreed to participate in this project—a truly international line-up. These experts, among them several of the world's leading Hogarth scholars, have uncovered much new material, leading to fresh insights into the artist and his work.

For instance, did you know that Hogarth's *Masquerades and Operas* is based on a German anti-Catholic propaganda print and that the dog depicted in his so-called *Self-Portrait with Pug* isn't really a pug at all? Are you acquainted with the narrative picture series by Continental artists that were published before Hogarth's birth and after his death? Did you know that Tom Rakewell of *A Rake's Progress* was expelled from Oxford for putting his bedmaker's daughter in the family way? Have you considered the madman trying to solve the problem of calculating longitude at sea in the last scene of the Rake series, or the formal structure of *A Midnight Modern Conversation*? One writer shows that Hogarth's *Night* includes several formal signifiers that ridicule some of the most socially prominent Freemasons of his day; another argues that *The Enraged Musician* seems to satirically represent a musical combat between two foreign musicians who were sacked by George Frideric Handel. One article discusses that *Marriage A-la-Mode* mocks Lord Squanderfield's paedophilia; another treats *The Gate of Calais* as a traditional mouth of hell scene that may include a caricature of Tobias Smollett. A contributor suggests that *The Four Stages of Cruelty* seems to sarcastically criticise the brutal practices of famous obstetricians and anatomists who didn't shrink from murdering fallen women and their unborn children in a quest for a greater understanding of female anatomy, and, somewhat cynically, improved obstetrical practice. Hogarth's conversation piece, *Captain Lord George Graham in his Cabin,* may include a hitherto unidentified placement of a self-portrait; and Isaac Newton's *Method of Fluxions* and the works of the marine painter, Peter Monamy, may have contributed to Hogarth's concept of the "Line of Beauty". Have you read academic essays on the language of dress or on the surviving architecture to be seen in several of Hogarth's works; or about the artist's shadowy widow Jane? Did you know that Hogarth made a caricature of Samuel Johnson portraying the learned doctor as an all too enthusiastic art lover, or that Hogarth's work was a considerable influence on Victorian art and still continues to be relevant to the teaching and practice of art?

If your imagination is twitched by these intriguing insights, then you are invited to read this book, which contains many more surprising insights upon William Hogarth and his work, life and times.

Table of Contents:

Introduction

I. Two Hogarthian Veterans looking back over their Work

II. Recent Views on either Single Works or the Series

III. Hogarth's Contribution to Portraiture

IV. Hogarth's Theory of Art: The Analysis of Beauty

VIII. The Artist's Influences on his Widow, the German Enlightenment and Victorian Art

IX. Hogarth and Art Education: then and now

Forthcoming Publication

Bernd W. Krysmanski

A Hogarth Bibliography

An Annotated Index on the Source Literature of
William Hogarth and his Works

Collated as an Interdisciplinary Research Tool

2 volumes

Georg Olms Verlag

Hildesheim · Zürich · New York

In 1997 the tercentenary of William Hogarth's birth was celebrated, and in 2014 the 250th anniversary of his death. It is high time for a comprehensive evaluation of the now considerable body of literature relating to the artist and his period, and for assembling an up-to-date bibliography of this work, systematically structured in index-fashion and, where feasible, fully annotated—a readily accessible commentary and source for citation.

Previous bibliographies are simply inadequate from today's point of view, and most publications on Hogarth include only short, select bibliographies or condensed entries in their "Abbreviations and Short Titles" keys. This bibliography will provide a practical resource for a range of users, including historians, art historians, literary historians, eighteenth-century experts, scholars in social and cultural studies, students, librarians, journalists and antiquarians, offering a readable and readily accessible guide to accurate information on specific works by Hogarth; written sources by or about the artist; subjects; themes; keywords or concepts, and more. This 2-volume reference book presents, as far as possible, all known art historical and literary sources; monographs; newspaper and journal articles; pamphlets; exhibition catalogues; theses; and other publications that have come to the compiler's notice, dating from the artist's lifetime up to the present.

It can be a frustrating waste of time to seek information on a specific picture by Hogarth or on related themes without a guide to the works by title—the works being, after all, the most likely point of departure for an enquiry. In most cases the information desired is widely scattered about in different publications and not readily identifiable. Accordingly this forthcoming bibliography not only includes an annotated alphabetical list of all written sources on the artist, but in volume 1 a list of the titles of all of Hogarth's works alphabetically arranged, each title having its own individual bibliography.

This research tool is also designed to stimulate new thinking about significant themes and topics in Hogarth's work and his times. Volume 2 is therefore aimed at those who wish to investigate more exhaustively specific subjects or names related to the artist. It is arranged thematically and relates to various matters concerning Hogarth's life; his art in general; his attitudes towards other artists and writers and the Old Masters; as well as the cultural and social background and criticism concerning his art. The numerous subheadings refer to different topics, for example, "Formal analysis of Hogarth's art"; "Hogarth the painter"; "Portraits by Hogarth"; "Hogarth's ancestry, name, and family"; "Hogarth's friends and enemies"; "Hogarth and Henry Fielding"; "Hogarth and Sir Joshua Reynolds"; "Hogarth's Dogs"; "Eroticism, Sexuality and Venereal Disease in Hogarth's art"; "The London theatre/Theatricality in Hogarth's art" and more.

The initial chapter of volume 2, entitled "Three Centuries of Scholarship on Hogarth", is possibly the most significant section of the entire bibliography, as the literature on Hogarth is here listed chronologically by author and may therefore be called a bibliography in its own right. Further subchapters deal with "Articles on Hogarth in Journals and Periodicals" and "Unpublished MA and PhD theses dealing with Hogarth"—alphabetical lists not to be found elsewhere.

This multifaceted reference tool promises to become an indispensable companion to all those who are interested in the enigmatic world of one of Britain's most fascinating artistic personalities, William Hogarth.